PRAYER HARVEST

Prayer to a Spiritual Man is What Oxygen is to a Natural Man

ABIMBOLA O. OLAGUNJU

Grosvenor House
Publishing Limited

The right of Abimbola O. Olagunju to be identified as the author of this
work has been asserted in accordance with Section 78
of the Copyright, Designs and Patents Act 1988

The book cover is copyright to Abimbola O. Olagunju

This book is published by
Grosvenor House Publishing Ltd
Link House
140 The Broadway, Tolworth, Surrey, KT6 7HT.
www.grosvenorhousepublishing.co.uk

This book is a work of fiction. Any resemblance to
people or events, past or present, is purely coincidental.

A CIP record for this book
is available from the British Library

ISBN 978-1-83975-298-8

PRAYER HARVEST

"For verily I say unto you, That whosoever shall say unto this mountain, Be thou removed, and be thou cast into the sea; and shall not doubt in his heart, but shall believe that those things which he saith shall come to pass; he shall have whatsoever he saith."
Mark 11:23

ABIMBOLA O. OLAGUNJU

CONTENTS

INTRODUCTION

Glory be to God and the Father of our Lord Jesus Christ, who has blessed us with all spiritual blessings in heavenly places. I bless the Lord for the opportunity to be a partaker of this gift.

I wrote this prayer book to address ignorance about prayer found in the body of Christ. The book teaches you to understand how to pray and to pray correctly. Prayer is a lifestyle of the believer, so you must know when to pray and how to pray. I trust the Lord that as you go through this book, your understanding will come back to life, your eyes of understanding will be enlightened, and you will increase in the knowledge of the word of God.

John taught his disciples how to pray; Jesus also did the same. As a believer, you need to be taught what to pray for and how to pray. Before the birth of Jesus, the Pharisees, Sadducees, and scribes had their formula for prayer, which today's church is practicing and celebrating. Throughout Jesus' ministry, He never killed anyone in His prayer. He rebuked His disciples when they brought the idea of calling down fire on a particular village.

Luke 9:54–56; "**54.** *And when his disciples James and John saw this, they said, Lord, wilt thou that we command fire to come down from heaven, and consume them, even as Elias did?* **55**. *But he turned, and rebuked them, and said, Ye know not what manner of Spirit ye are of.* **56**. *For the Son of man is not come to destroy men's lives, but to save them. And they went to another village.*" (KJV).

Apostle Paul never called down fire to roast anyone or to destroy anyone's life. Paul said to Timothy in **2 Timothy 2:15**; "**15**. *Study to shew thyself approved unto God, a workman that needeth not to be ashamed, rightly dividing the word of truth*" (KJV). Until a believer can rightly divide the word of truth, the believer will remain ignorant of God's word. Jesus is your example for a Christian race. So, follow Jesus' doctrine. Salvation indeed defines God's purpose for humanity, and upon believing the gospel, you are to grow and walk in the knowledge of salvation. You are to continue to learn and follow instructions and lay down doctrines in your walk with God.

1 Timothy 2:1–4; *"***1***. I exhort therefore, that, first of all, supplications, prayers, intercessions, and giving of thanks, be made for all men;* **2**. *For kings, and for all that are in authority; that we may lead a quiet and peaceable life in all godliness and honesty.* **3**. *For this is good and acceptable in the sight of God our Saviour;* **4**. *Who will have all men to be saved, and to come unto the knowledge of the truth"* (KJV).

Jesus had the twelve disciples, as they were men learning from Jesus. One thing Jesus taught his disciples was how to pray. Jesus taught his disciples not to pray for earthly things in **Luke 11:1–2**; *"***1**. *And it came to pass, that, as he was praying in a certain place, when he ceased, one of his disciples said unto him, Lord, teach us to pray, as John also taught his disciples.* **2**. *And he said unto them, when ye pray, say, Our Father which art in heaven, Hallowed be thy name. Thy kingdom come. Thy will be done, as in heaven, so in earth, "* (KJV).

He also taught them not to pray for earthly things in **Matthew 6:9–13**; *"***9**. *After this manner therefore pray ye: Our Father which art in heaven, Hallowed be thy name.* **10**. *Thy kingdom come. Thy will be done in earth, as it is in heaven.* **11**. *Give us this day our daily bread.* **12**. *And forgive us our debts, as we forgive our debtors.* **13**. *And lead us not* *into temptation, but deliver us from evil: For thine is the kingdom, and the power, and the glory, forever. Amen"* (KJV). In **Luke 11:1–2** and **Matthew 6:9–13**, Jesus changed the disciple's mindset and pattern of prayers by drawing their attention to the things of the kingdom of God. **Matthew 6:33**; *"But seek ye first the kingdom of God, and his righteousness; and all these things shall be added unto you"* (KJV). It is not because you seek the kingdom that everything will be added unto you.

      Matthew 6:25–32; *"25. Therefore I say unto you, Take no thought for your life, what ye shall eat, or what ye shall drink; nor yet for your body, what ye shall put on. Is not the life more than meat, and the body than raiment? 26. Behold the fowls of the air: for they sow not, neither do they reap, nor gather into barns; yet your heavenly Father feedeth them. Are ye not much better than they? 27. Which of you by taking thought can add one cubit unto his stature? 28. And why take ye thought for raiment? Consider the lilies of the field, how they grow; they toil not, neither do they spin: 29. And yet I say unto you, That even Solomon in all his glory was not arrayed like one of these. 30. Wherefore, if God so clothe the grass of the field, which today is, and tomorrow is cast into the oven, shall he not much more clothe you, O ye of little faith? 31. Therefore take no thought, saying, What shall we eat? or, What shall*

we drink? or, Wherewithal shall we be clothed?
32. *(For after all these things do the Gentiles seek:)*
for your heavenly Father knoweth that ye have need
of all these things" (KJV).

From the book of **Matthew 6:25–32**,
unbelievers (Gentiles) seek after earthly things. A
man does not need to believe the gospel to have such
material things. The believer is meant to ask for what
is everlasting, which is found in Christ Jesus.

Mathew 7: 7–11; *"7. Ask, and it shall be*
given you; seek, and ye shall find; knock, and it shall
be opened unto you: **8.** *For every one that asketh*
receiveth; and he that seeketh findeth; and to him
that knocketh it shall be opened. **9.** *Or what man is*
there of you, whom if his son ask bread, will he give
him a stone? **10.** *Or if he ask a fish, will he give him*
a serpent? **11.** *If ye then, being evil, know how to*
give good gifts unto your children, how much more
shall your Father which is in heaven give good
things to them that ask him?" (KJV).

The true riches of a believer are not how
many things he possesses but how much of the
revelation of Jesus, the believer has; in **Luke 12:15**;
"And he said unto them, Take heed, and beware of
covetousness: for a man's life consisteth not in the
abundance of the things which he possesseth"
(KJV).

1 Timothy 6:6; *"But godliness with*
contentment is great gain. **7.** *For we brought nothing*

into this world, and it is certain we can carry nothing out. **8.** *And having food and raiment let us be therewith content.* **9.** *But they that will be rich fall into temptation and a snare, and into many foolish and hurtful lusts, which drown men in destruction and perdition.* **10.** *For the love of money is the root of all evil: which while some coveted after, they have erred from the faith, and pierced themselves through with many sorrows.* **11.** *But thou, O man of God, flee these things; and follow after righteousness, godliness, faith, love, patience, meekness.* **12.** *Fight the good fight of faith, lay hold on eternal life, whereunto thou art also called, and hast professed a good profession before many witnesses"* (KJV).

Jesus taught his disciples what to pray for and what not to pray for. Let us examine what Brother Paul wrote in **Ephesians 1:16–23**; "**16.** *Cease not to give thanks for you, making mention of you in my prayers;* **17.** *That the God of our Lord Jesus Christ, the Father of glory, may give unto you the spirit of wisdom and revelation in the knowledge of him:* **18.** *The eyes of your understanding being enlightened; that ye may know what is the hope of his calling, and what the riches of the glory of his inheritance in the saints,* **19.** *And what is the exceeding greatness of his power to us-ward who believe, according to the working of his mighty power,* **20.** *Which he wrought in Christ, when he raised him from the dead, and set him at his own* *right hand in the heavenly places,* **21.** *Far above all principality, and power, and might, and dominion, and every name that is named, not only in this world, but also in that which is to come:* **22.** *And hath put all things under his feet, and gave him to be the head over all things to the church,* **23.** *Which is his body, the fullness of him that filleth all in all"* (KJV).

In **verse 18**, Paul prayed the believers to understand the hope of their calling, the riches of God's inheritance in the saints. Paul's prayers in his epistles focused on knowledge and not material things; **Philippians 1:9**; *"And this I pray, that your love may abound yet more and more in knowledge and in all judgment;* **10.** *That ye may approve things that are excellent; that ye may be sincere and without offence till the day of Christ;* **11.** *Being filled with the fruits of righteousness, which are by Jesus Christ, unto the glory and praise of God"* (KJV).

Colossians 1:9; *"For this cause we also, since the day we heard it, do not cease to pray for you, and to desire that ye might be filled with the knowledge of his will in all wisdom and spiritual understanding;* **10.** *That ye might walk worthy of the Lord unto all pleasing, being fruitful in every good work, and increasing in the knowledge of God;* **11.** *Strengthened with all might, according to his glorious power, unto all patience and longsuffering with joyfulness"* (KJV). Hence adequate reading is critical for learning. Reading will involve a careful and diligent approach to understand the words used and how they are used.

The Subject of Prayer

Some believers think prayer; they imagine it. Some believers often are found wishing or imagining prayer, not knowing they are not communicating with God. For instance, a believer might be desiring something say – a car; this is just a wish/desire that is being thought out or spoken and imagined in the mind of the individual, but that is not prayer. Prayer is not imagination. When you imagine you are praying in your consciousness, you are not really communicating with God. Prayer involves verbalizing our desires, to speak forth our request unto God. **Luke 11:2**; *"And he said unto them, When ye pray, **say**, Our Father which art in heaven, Hallowed be thy name. Thy kingdom come. Thy will be done, as in heaven, so in earth"* (KJV).

*"… When ye pray, **say**…"* not wish or desire. In **Mark 11:23**; *"For verily I say unto you, That whosoever shall **say** unto this mountain, Be thou removed, and be thou cast into the sea; and shall not doubt in his heart, but shall believe that those things which he **saith** shall come to pass; he shall have whatsoever he **saith"*** (KJV). Notice the words **say, saith, saith** in one verse, connoting emphasis.

James 1:5, *"If any of you lack wisdom, let him **ask** of God, that giveth to all men liberally, and*

upbraideth not; and it shall be given him" (KJV).
Matthew 21:22; *"And all things, whatsoever ye shall **ask** in prayer, believing, ye shall receive"* (KJV). God expects that we make a request; He wants us to ask him. And you **ask** by speaking not by imagination and thinking. **Mark 11:24**; *"Therefore I say unto you, What things so ever ye desire, when ye pray, believe that ye receive them, and ye shall have them"* (KJV). Prayer is saying or talking. Prayer is making your desires known to the Father through spoken words, not thoughts or desires. It also means to make a strong appeal or fixed request of what you desire. Making a fixed request implies that prayer cannot be carried out by thinking but by spoken words. It is an activity carried out in reverence by man.

Philippians 4:6; *"Be careful for nothing; but in everything by prayer and supplication with thanksgiving let your requests be made known unto God"* (KJV). The word prayer and supplication refer to the same thing: making petitions or coming before a higher authority with your request. By prayer and supplication, let your request (*appeal, plea, petition*) be made known unto God. In prayer, two parties are involved – the asker (*receiver*) and the giver (*God*). In communication, you must speak with your mouth and sometimes be audible. You do not imagine it or be silent and assume the other party is hearing your thoughtful request. You must be focused, devoid of distraction in the act of praying. Speak out the words in the place of prayer. For instance, when Hannah spoke in her heart, her lips still moved. **1 Samuel 1:13**; *"Now Hannah, she spake in her heart; only her lips moved, but her voice was not heard: therefore Eli thought she had been drunken"* (KJV).

That means there are no outstanding answers to prayers without first an exceptional preparation in the heart. God does not reckon with the outward appearance or physical efforts; what moves Him is your heart. Therefore, your heart must be set for an encounter with Him when you pray. Preparing your heart in purity is the first step to establishing a viable communication link with God because prayer flows well when sin is absent. You may be going to church, but that does not necessarily make you a believer or born again. Sin is a barrier to prayers. So, an individual must accept the gift of God (salvation) to all men.

Redemption will open a better communication link between a son (believer) and the Father (God). Prayer is not just reporting your case to God; it is communicating with him. Every genuine discussion or dialogue involves comments, inquiries and responses from the parties involved. It should be a two-way communication flow. But most people do all the talking in prayer, not giving God a chance to speak to them in return, nor pausing to listen to what he has to say. Believers should engage in responsive meditational prayers. **Jeremiah 33:3**; *"Call unto* *me, and I will answer thee, and shew thee great and mighty things, which thou knowest not"* (KJV). Therefore, we can boldly say, prayer is a fellowship born out of a relationship.

When you approach God in prayer, one of the things you must guard against is offenses. Many believers are offended in God, and all they do in prayer is nothing except to complain. They justify themselves against God, saying, *"Lord, I have done everything that you commanded; I have paid my tithe, and I have given more than everyone in my local church. Only you (God) haven't done your part"*. They count themselves faithful and God otherwise. *"Anything that moves you to murmur against God is moving you against your destiny"*. **Isaiah 45:9**; *"Woe unto him that striveth with his Maker! Let the potsherd strive with the potsherds of the earth. Shall the clay say to him that fashioneth it, What makest thou? or thy work, He hath no hands?"* (KJV).

You do not approach God in prayer, based on your qualification, but because he has qualified you in Christ. **Luke 18:10**; *"Two men went up into the temple to pray; the one a Pharisee, and the other a publican.* **11.** *The Pharisee stood and prayed thus with himself, God, I thank thee, that I am not as other men are, extortioners, unjust, adulterers, or even as this publican.* **12.** *I fast twice in the week, I give tithes of all that I possess.* **13.** *And the publican,* *standing afar off, would not lift up so much as his eyes unto heaven, but smote upon his breast, saying, God be merciful to me a sinner.* **14.** *I tell you, this man went down to his house justified rather than the other: for every one that exalteth himself shall be abased; and he that humbleth himself shall be exalted"* (KJV).

Colossians 1:12; *"Giving thanks unto the Father, which hath made us meet to be partakers of the inheritance of the saints in light"* (KJV).

So, set your heart right before him. Count God faithful in **all** things. Refuse to complain and murmur, instead let God know that you have no alternative (substitute) besides Him. Tell Him that you are ready to wait until your answer comes from Him. Brother Paul said, *"16. And herein do I exercise myself, to have always a conscience void of offence toward God, and toward men,"* **(Acts 24:16)** (KJV). That is the way to maintain a good communication line with the Father.

Your effectiveness as a believer in prayer is a function of your understanding of every good thing you possess in Christ Jesus. It will be erroneous to assume that every believer knows how to pray and what prayer entails, which is why prayer must be properly taught and understood from the scriptures. So, the subject of prayer must not be learned through experience but from the scriptures. In other words, the scriptures are your only authority in teaching every Christian practice, including prayer. In examining the subject of prayer, your authority lies solely in the scriptures, particularly the epistles. The essence of teaching the theme of 'prayer harvest' is to bring about effectiveness in the place of prayer.

CHAPTER ONE

PRAYER IS A CONTINUOUS ACT

EPHESIANS 6:18

"Praying always with all prayer and supplication in the
Spirit, and watching thereunto with all perseverance and
supplication for all saints;" (KJV)

Paul said to pray always, making
known your desires and request to
the Lord. Prayer should be a daily
routine and a lifestyle of the
believer. Jesus had this lifestyle, and His disciples
followed the same lifestyle, even after His
resurrection and ascension. **Acts 1:12–14**; "**12**. *Then*

returned they unto Jerusalem from the mount called Olivet, which is from Jerusalem a sabbath day's journey. **13.** *And when they were come in, they went up into an upper room, where abode both Peter, and James, and John, and Andrew, Philip, and Thomas, Bartholomew, and Matthew, James the son of Alphaeus, and Simon Zelotes, and Judas the brother of James.* **14.** *These all continued with one accord in prayer and supplication, with the women, and Mary the mother of Jesus, and with his brethren"* (KJV).

Prayer became their lifestyle, constant (praying continuously), and there was never a point when prayer became invalid or insignificant. **Acts 2:42**; *"And they continued stedfastly in the apostles' doctrine and fellowship, and in breaking of bread, and in prayers".* **Acts 3:1**; *"Now Peter and John went up together into the temple at the hour of prayer, being the ninth hour"* (KJV). **Acts 4:31**; *"And when they had prayed, the place was shaken where they were assembled together; and they were all filled with the Holy Ghost, and they spake the word of God with boldness"* (KJV). **Acts 6:4**; *"But we will give ourselves continually to prayer, and to the ministry of the word"* (KJV).

Romans 12:12; *"Rejoicing in hope; patient in tribulation; continuing (constant) instant in prayer"* (KJV). **Colossians 4:2**; *"Continue in prayer, and watch in the same with thanksgiving"*

(KJV). In his Epistles (Letters) to the Romans and the Colossians, Apostle Paul admonished them to pray. Also, Jesus instructed His disciples to pray always. **Luke 21:36**; *"Watch ye therefore, and pray always, that ye may be accounted worthy to escape all these things that shall come to pass, and to stand before the Son of man"* (KJV). As a born-again Christian, prayer should be your lifestyle. Give yourself to prayer continually and make your request known unto the Father. **1 Thessalonians 5:17**; *"Pray without ceasing"* (KJV).

Prayer is an exercise done daily and continuously. There is never a time a believer stops praying. The different categories of things and people you pray for, imply that a believer's life is a life of prayer. In praying for yourself, you should pray much more for your spiritual wellbeing, for insight into God's word more than material things as this was the emphasis in scriptures.

Ephesians 1:16–23; *"***16.** *Cease not to give thanks for you, making mention of you in my prayers;* **17.** *That the God of our Lord Jesus Christ, the Father of glory, may give unto you the Spirit of wisdom and revelation in the knowledge of him:* **18.** *The eyes of your understanding being enlightened; that ye may know what is the hope of his calling, and what the riches of the glory of his inheritance in the saints,* **19.** *And what is the exceeding greatness of his power to us-ward who believe, according to the* *working of his mighty power,* **20.** *Which he wrought in Christ, when he raised him from the dead, and set him at his own right hand in the heavenly places,* **21.** *Far above all principality, and power, and might, and dominion, and every name that is named, not only in this world, but also in that which is to come:* **22.** *And hath put all things under his feet, and gave him to be the head over all things to the church,* **23.** *Which is his body, the fulness of him that filleth all in all"* (KJV).

You are also to pray for yourself to walk in God's plans and purpose for your life and walk in wisdom. **James 1:5**; *"If any of you lack wisdom, let him ask of God, that giveth to all men liberally, and upbraideth not; and it shall be given him"* (KJV). As a true believer, you should be praying more for others, especially other believers. You should spend more time praying for your local church, the members, and ministers of the church.

What is Prayer?

As simple as the question may seem, not every believer knows what prayer is or what it entails. Answering this question will help the believer to be effective in prayer. *Prayer is fellowship.* **John 17: 9, 20**; *"9. I pray for them: I pray not for the world, but for them which thou hast given me; for they are thine". and "20. Neither pray*

I for these alone, but for them also which shall believe in me through their word" (KJV).

Jesus prayed because of the desire to commune with the Father as a sign of devotion. He was not praying for an immediate need. He prayed as a sign of fellowship with the Father. So, prayer is a fellowship. Prayer is fellowshipping with the Father of Spirits in the Spirit. It is not a soulish (mental) affair but a spiritual affair of fellowship with God. Prayer is a spiritual walk, a relationship, and a communion between the heart of man and God. Prayer should not be limited to the time you have your quiet time alone. Prayer should be an attitude you maintain throughout the day.

Prayer is the respiration of a spiritual man. Prayer to a spiritual man is what oxygen is to a natural man. As a natural man cannot survive without breathing in air or oxygen, a spiritual man cannot survive without prayer. It is indeed good to be busy for God. Still, it is even better to be occupied with God. **2 Corinthians 3:18**; *"But we all, with open face beholding as in a glass the glory of the Lord, are changed into the same image from glory to glory, even as by the Spirit of the Lord"* (KJV). Prayer is the invisible spiritual cable through which God's power flows. **Isaiah 40:31**; *"But they that wait upon the Lord shall renew their strength; they shall mount up with wings as eagles;*

they shall run, and not be weary; and they shall walk, and not faint" (KJV).

For instance, there will be no power supply from the electric power station to the customers without distribution cables. Likewise, prayer is the power supply cable to the believer's spiritual wellbeing. Your prayer connects you to God, thereby making His unlimited power available in your life and situations. So, a prayerless believer is a powerless believer. When you pray, you make power available which goes to work to arrange and re-arrange things – **James 5:16** *"Confess your faults one to another, and pray one for another, that ye may be healed. The effectual fervent prayer of a righteous man availeth much* (KJV).

In the New Testament, prayer was translated from the Greek, which implies to come before a higher authority to ask (*to make a request*). To appear before a higher power means prayer should be done with a sense of reverence. Prayer was also used in the following Bible texts for coming before God to pray. **Luke 6:12**; *"And it came to pass in those days, that he went out into a mountain to pray, and continued all night in **prayer** to God"* (KJV). **Philippians 1:9**; *"And this I pray, that your love may abound yet more and more in knowledge and in all judgment"* (KJV). **Ephesians 6:18**; *"Praying always with all prayer and supplication in the Spirit, and watching thereunto with all perseverance and* *supplication for all saints"* (KJV). **Colossians 1:3**; *"We give thanks to God and the Father of our Lord Jesus Christ, praying always for you,"* (KJV). **1 Thessalonians 5:17**; *"Pray without ceasing".* **Philippians 4:6**; *"Be careful for nothing; but in everything by prayer and supplication with thanksgiving let your requests be made known unto God"* (KJV). **Act 12:5**; *"Peter therefore was kept in prison: but prayer was made without ceasing of the church unto God for him"* (KJV).

Romans 15:30; *"Now I beseech you, brethren, for the Lord Jesus Christ's sake, and for the love of the Spirit, that ye strive together with me in your prayers to God for me"* (KJV). The New Testament text reveals that prayer involves ***God*** and ***man***. Men are the ones that pray to God. Note that the attitude of a believer in prayer is essential. The attitude is the basis for the word supplication, which speaks of a humble request involving a fixed demand with a profound obeisance. The heartfelt prayer and supplication of a righteous man make power available and able to do/carry out changes – **James 5:16**; *"Confess your faults one to another, and pray one for another, that ye may be healed. The effectual fervent prayer of a righteous man availeth much"* (KJV). Paul's prayer was for the church, the local church. You can pray in the Spirit always, daily, without ceasing. You are edified when everyone is growing and participating actively in the church.

7

Your prayer lifestyle should be done in the Spirit, praying in *tongues (i.e. Praying in the Spirit)*.

Speaking in Tongues (Praying in the Spirit)

As a believer, you are to embrace the art and culture of praying in the Spirit. You already have the Holy Spirit indwelling when you got saved. Being in the Spirit implies being in Christ. **Ephesians 1:13**; *"In whom ye also trusted, after that ye heard the word of truth, the gospel of your salvation: in whom also after that ye believed, ye were sealed with that holy Spirit of promise,* **14**. *Which is the earnest of our inheritance until the redemption of the purchased possession, unto the praise of his glory* (KJV).

Romans 8:1–10; *"***1.** *There is therefore now no condemnation to them which are in Christ Jesus, who walk not after the flesh, but after the Spirit.* **2.** *For the law of the Spirit of life in Christ Jesus hath made me free from the law of sin and death.* **3.** *For what the law could not do, in that it was weak through the flesh, God sending his own Son in the likeness of sinful flesh, and for sin, condemned sin in the flesh:* **4.** *That the righteousness of the law might be fulfilled in us, who walk not after the flesh, but after the Spirit.* **5.** *For they that are after the flesh do mind the things of the flesh; but they that are after the Spirit the things of the Spirit.* **6.** *For to be carnally minded is death; but to be spiritually minded is life* *and peace. 7. Because the carnal mind is enmity against God: for it is not subject to the law of God, neither indeed can be. 8. So then they that are in the flesh cannot please God. 9. But ye are not in the flesh, but in the Spirit, if so be that the Spirit of God dwell in you. Now if any man have not the Spirit of Christ, he is none of his. 10. And if Christ be in you, the body is dead because of sin; but the Spirit is life because of righteousness"* (KJV).

Observe that the book of Romans 8:1–10 emphasis was on the believer being in union with praying in the Spirit. You are introduced by apostle Paul to a pattern of prayer in the New Testament called praying in the spirit *(speaking in tongues)* because you are born of the spirit. **John 3:6**; *"That which is born of the flesh is flesh; and that which is born of the Spirit is spirit"* (KJV).

Praying in the spirit is an activity that is dependent on the believer's position and status in Christ Jesus. **1 Corinthians 14:2–18, 39**; *"2. For he that speaketh in an unknown tongue speaketh not unto men, but unto God: for no man understandeth him; howbeit in the Spirit he speaketh mysteries... 14. For if I pray in an unknown tongue, my Spirit prayeth, but my understanding is unfruitful. 15. What is it then? I will pray with the Spirit, and I will pray with the understanding also: I will sing with the Spirit, and I will sing with the understanding also... 18. I thank my God, I speak with tongues more than*

9

*ye all". "**39.** Wherefore, brethren, covet to prophesy, and forbid not to speak with tongues"* (KJV).

Apostle Paul admonishes the believer *(you)* not to forbid speaking in tongues. A man cannot understand the meaning when one prays in tongues until it is interpreted. *"For he that speaketh in an unknown tongue speaketh not unto men, but unto God: for no man understandeth him; howbeit in the spirit he speaketh mysteries"*. Paul also encourages individuals and the church to pray in the spirit because it is the only way to pray effectively.

Benefits of Praying in Tongues

1 Corinthians 14:4; *"He that speaketh in an unknown tongue **edifieth himself**; but he that prophesieth edifieth the church... **17.** For thou verily **givest thanks well**, but the other is not edified"*. When you give worship in the spirit, you worship well. **Jude 1:20**; *"But ye, beloved, **building up yourselves** on your most holy faith, praying in the Holy Ghost,"* According to **1 Corinthians 14:4** and **Jude 1:20**, when you pray in the spirit, you edify yourself, strengthening, and building up your spirituality. Praying in the spirit gives the believer an advantage because the believer prays from the position of authority, exercising your power here on earth.

Ephesians 1:19–23; *"19. And what is the exceeding greatness of his power to us-ward who believe, according to the working of his mighty power,* **20.** *Which he wrought in Christ, when he raised him from the dead, and set him at his own right hand in the heavenly places,* **21.** *Far above all principality, and power, and might, and dominion, and every name that is named, not only in this world, but also in that which is to come:* **22.** *And hath put all things under his feet, and gave him to be the head over all things to the church,* **23.** *Which is his body, the fulness of him that filleth all in all"* (KJV). **Ephesians 2:5, 6**; *"5. Even when we were dead in sins, hath quickened us together with Christ, (by grace ye are saved;)* **6.** *And hath raised us up together, and made us sit together in heavenly places in Christ Jesus:"* (KJV).

Praying in the Spirit is what the believers do for being in Christ. Praying in tongues was a common phenomenon in the Epistles. One might want to ask; ***is it possible to make a request while speaking in tongues?*** **Ephesians 6:18**; *"Praying always with **all prayer and supplication in the Spirit** and watching thereunto with all perseverance and supplication for all saints"* (KJV). All manner of request can be made while praying in tongues. These requests could include praying for men (*especially believers*), situations (*circumstances*) or things.

How is Praying in Tongues Done?

As you pray in the spirit, you are praying in the knowledge of the demands. **1 Corinthians 14:14, 15**; *"14. For if I pray in an unknown tongue, my Spirit prayeth, but my understanding is unfruitful. 15. What is it then? I will pray with the Spirit, and I will pray with the understanding also: I will sing with the Spirit, and I will sing with the understanding also"* (KJV). Hence, you may not understand when you pray in an unknown tongue; but you pray with the mind when you pray in the Spirit. Brother Paul must have expressed his desires in prayer for the church's saints by praying in the Spirit (e.g. the church at Ephesus). **1 Corinthians 14:18**; *"I thank my God, I speak with tongues more than ye all"* (KJV).

Ephesians 1:16; *"Cease not to give thanks for you, making mention of you in my prayers; 17. That the God of our Lord Jesus Christ, the Father of glory, may give unto you the Spirit of wisdom and revelation in the knowledge of him: 18. The eyes of your understanding being enlightened; that ye may know what is the hope of his calling, and what the riches of the glory of his inheritance in the saints, 19. And what is the exceeding greatness of his power to us-ward who believe, according to the working of his mighty power, 20. Which he wrought in Christ,* *when he raised him from the dead, and set him at his own right hand in the heavenly places,"* (KJV).

The believer is not limited to a place to pray as practiced under the Old Testament, where they go to the temple to pray. Instead, the believer can pray at any time in any area because the believer is the house of prayer. Jesus said to the Woman at the well in **John 4:1–24**; *"... 20. Our fathers worshipped in this mountain; and ye say, that in Jerusalem is the place where men ought to worship. 21. Jesus saith unto her, Woman, believe me, the hour cometh, when ye shall neither in this mountain, nor yet at Jerusalem, worship the Father... 23. But **the hour cometh, and now is, when the true worshippers shall worship the Father in Spirit and in truth**: for the Father seeketh such to worship him. 24. **God is a Spirit**: and they that worship him must worship him in Spirit and in truth"* (KJV).

Jesus was saying that now there is no particular place to go to worship the Father. A believer can worship Him anywhere because He dwells in you. When you pray in tongues, you pray for all believers. Praying in tongues enables you to withstand the enemy's wiles, persecution, and opposition against the gospel. It is essential to know that you are praying for more than one person when you pray in tongues and building yourself. Praying in tongues enhances you for the furtherance of the gospel. It is for believers to be strong, bold, and brave. You can take care of a believer's spiritual deficiencies when you pray in the Spirit. So, by praying, you supply strength for the believer's work against the enemy's wiles. You do not need to have a prayer point before you can pray in tongues.

Why Do Believers Pray?

You are taught to pray when the challenges of life seem overwhelming (**James 5:13**); *"Is any among you afflicted? let him pray. Is any merry? let him sing psalms"* (KJV). Prayer itself is more important than the things you get from it. There are things you pray for that you get by prayer that some other people do not pray about because they already have those things. That proves that it is not the earthly thing that is of utmost importance, but the prayer itself.

Prayer changes things (*circumstances, situations, conditions*), but the essential element that prayer change is the believer. Prayer is more about you (*the believer*) than what you are praying to receive. You ought to know that prayer causes you to change in attitude and thinking, enabling you to walk more in God's plan and purpose for your life. Prayer also changes your desires and resets your priorities.

Take a clue from Jesus at the mount of transfiguration in **Mathew 17:1, 2**; *"1. And after* *six days Jesus taketh Peter, James, and John his brother, and bringeth them up into an high mountain apart,* **2.** *And was transfigured before them: and his face did shine as the sun, and his raiment was white as the light"* (KJV). Jesus was transfigured, and His face did shine as the sun and raiment (*clothing*) was white as the light. The most important thing that prayer affects is the believer. You need to pray because prayer is your communion with your Father, enabling you and your Father to talk.

"Father, I adore you. You are a great father. I love you, Father. Thank you for loving me even when I didn't deserve it. My heart is glad to know what you have done for me; you cleansed me, you purified me, you sanctified me. Father open my eyes, let me understand the things you have done for me…" that is prayer.

Why do believers pray? … Believers pray because it is the *ongoing work* of Christ. There is the *finished work*, and there is the *unfinished work*. The ongoing works are prayer, study, ministry, spiritual growth, and renewal of the mind. The *unfinished work* centers on evangelism and giving. On *evangelism* (which is the *unfinished work*), Jesus rose from the dead (*after He finished the work*), He commanded us, saying go into the world and tell them what I have done. On *giving*, the gospel of Christ is amplified through your monetary contribution (*giving*). In giving, you must understand that you are not giving to receive something in return (*to get something*), you are giving because He has done it for you. So, the *ongoing* and *unfinished work* is the believers' responsibility to take delivery of what the finished work has provided through prayer.

The Power of Prayer

Prayer is an important theme taught in the Bible. It has a significant emphasis on the scriptures both by precepts and practice. Hence it is a subject that demands proper explanation like every other topic in the Christian tradition. It will be presumptuous to say all Christians know the real reasons why they need to pray and the power inherent in prayer. Even though you often pray and associate yourself with those who pray, you must know why you pray. Recognizing why you pray will enable you to pray with understanding, depth, regularity, and results.

Luke 11:1; "*And it came to pass, that, as he was praying in a certain place, when he ceased, one of his disciples said unto him, Lord, teach us to pray, as John also taught his disciples*" (KJV). The word disciple implies a student, one that follows a specific set of laid down principles. Also, disciple means learning and being accustomed to a belief or practice. Jesus beckoned the disciples to teach them how to pray, as John also taught his disciples. Jesus then gave instructions concerning 'prayer'.

Other exhortations and teachings on prayer in the epistles include **1Thessalonian 5:17** *Pray without ceasing.* **Ephesians 6:18** *Praying always with all prayer and supplication in the Spirit, and watching thereunto with all perseverance and supplication for all saints;* **Philippian 4:6** *Be careful for nothing; but in every thing by prayer and supplication with thanksgiving let your requests be made known unto God* (KJV).

Main Purpose of Prayer

The primary purposes of prayer designed by God are *for fellowship with God, receiving from God,* and *for spiritual warfare.* All other functions of prayer take their bearing from them.

Fellowship with God. Hebrews 11:5, 6; *"5. By faith Enoch was translated that he should not see death; and was not found, because God had translated him: for before his translation he had this testimony, that he pleased God. 6. But without faith it is impossible to please him: for he that cometh to God must believe that he is, and that he is a rewarder of them that diligently seek him"* (KJV).

Receiving from God, Mathew 7: 7 and James 4:2; *"7. Ask, and it shall be given you; seek,* *and ye shall find; knock, and it shall be opened unto you:".* and *"2. Ye lust, and have not: ye kill, and desire to have, and cannot obtain: ye fight and war, yet ye have not, because ye ask not."* (KJV).

Spiritual Warfare. Ephesians 6:10–18 and Mathew 18:18; *"10. Finally, my brethren, be strong in the Lord, and in the power of his might. 11. Put on the whole armour of God, that ye may be able to stand against the wiles of the devil. 12. For we wrestle not against flesh and blood, but against principalities, against powers, against the rulers of the darkness of this world, against spiritual wickedness in high places. 13. Wherefore take unto you the whole armour of God, that ye may be able to withstand in the evil day, and having done all, to stand. 14. Stand therefore, having your loins girt about with truth, and having on the breastplate of righteousness; 15. And your feet shod with the preparation of the gospel of peace; 16. Above all, taking the shield of faith, wherewith ye shall be able to quench all the fiery darts of the wicked. 17. And take the helmet of salvation, and the sword of the Spirit, which is the word of God: 18. Praying always with all prayer and supplication in the Spirit, and watching thereunto with all perseverance and supplication for all saints"* (KJV). **Matthew 18:18**; *"18. "Verily I say unto you, Whatsoever ye shall bind on earth shall be bound in heaven: and* *whatsoever ye shall loose on earth shall be loosed in heaven"* (KJV).

The Potency of Prayer

Prayer must be a significant spiritual phenomenon since prayer and fasting are practiced in all religions. You see God in the scriptures always demanding and commanding his people to pray. In response, you found that the most eminent men and women of God have been people who were fervent in prayer. The importance of prayer in a believer's life includes *prayer is the natural heart cry of man to his creator for things beneficial to his sustenance on earth. It is like a child to mother cry.* **Psalm 42:1–2**; *"1. As the hart panteth after the water brooks, so panteth my soul after thee, O God. 2. My soul thirsteth for God, for the living God: when shall I come and appear before God?"* (KJV). Prayer helps you to live and walk in the realm of the supernatural and brings intervention **(Acts 12)**. Also, prayer changes hopeless situations **(2 Kings 20:1–6)**.

Prayer is an antidote against worry, anxiety, surfeiting, drunkenness, and cares of this life. **Philippians 4:6–7**; *"6. Be careful for nothing; but in everything by prayer and supplication with thanksgiving let your requests be made known unto God. 7. And the peace of God, which passeth all understanding, shall keep your hearts and minds*

through Christ Jesus." (KJV). **Luke 21:34–36**; *"34.
And take heed to yourselves, lest at any time your
hearts be overcharged with surfeiting, and
drunkenness, and cares of this life, and so that day
come upon you unawares. 35. For as a snare shall it
come on all them that dwell on the face of the whole
earth. 36. Watch ye therefore, and pray always, that
ye may be accounted worthy to escape all these
things that shall come to pass, and to stand before the
Son of man"* (KJV).

Prayer generates holy emotions, the right
attitude, and righteous disposition in your soul. It
brings God's peace to a troubled mind in a troubled
world. Prayer is still the main business of your Lord
in Heaven. **Hebrews 7:25**; *"Wherefore he is able
also to save them to the uttermost that come unto
God by him, seeing **he ever liveth to make
intercession for them.**"* (KJV). As He is in heaven,
so you should be on earth. His concern and burden
must be the concern and responsibility of the
church. *We pray so that God may provide more
laborer for the salvation of fellow human beings.*
Mathew 9:36; *"But when he saw the multitudes,
he was moved with compassion on them, because
they fainted, and were scattered abroad, as sheep
having no shepherd".*

Prayer guarantees victory in spiritual
warfare. **Exodus 17:8–15**; *"8. Then came Amalek,
and fought with Israel in Rephidim. 9. And Moses*

said unto Joshua, Choose us out men, and go out, fight with Amalek: tomorrow I will stand on the top of the hill with the rod of God in mine hand. **10.** *So Joshua did as Moses had said to him, and fought with Amalek: and Moses, Aaron, and Hur went up to the top of the hill.* **11.** *And it came to pass, when Moses held up his hand, that Israel prevailed: and when he let down his hand, Amalek prevailed.* **12.** *But Moses' hands were heavy; and they took a stone, and put it under him, and he sat thereon; and Aaron and Hur stayed up his hands, the one on the one side, and the other on the other side; and his hands were steady until the going down of the sun.* **13.** *And Joshua discomfited Amalek and his people with the edge of the sword.* **14.** *And the Lord said unto Moses, Write this for a memorial in a book, and rehearse it in the ears of Joshua: for I will utterly put out the remembrance of Amalek from under heaven.* **15.** *And Moses built an altar, and called the name of it Jehovah-nissi:"* (KJV).

Prayer raises a standard against all enemies of God and the gospel. **Daniel 4; Acts 12** and **Isaiah 59:19**; *"So shall they fear the name of the LORD from the west, and his glory from the rising of the sun. When the enemy shall come in like a flood, the Spirit of the LORD shall lift up a standard against him"* (KJV). Prayer brings power and strength to a weak life. **Isaiah 40:31**; *"But they that wait upon the LORD shall renew their strength; they shall mount* *up with wings as eagles; they shall run, and not be weary; and they shall walk, and not faint"* (KJV). **Acts 4:31, 33**; *"***31.** *And when they had prayed, the place was shaken where they were assembled together; and they were all filled with the Holy Ghost, and they spake the word of God with boldness.* **33.** *And with great power gave the apostles witness of the resurrection of the Lord Jesus: and great grace was upon them all"* (KJV).

CHAPTER TWO
HOW TO PRAY
EPHESIANS 6:18

"Praying always with all prayer and supplication in the Spirit, and watching thereunto with all perseverance and supplication for all saints;" (KJV)

It says, *"Praying always with all prayer and supplication **in the Spirit**..."*. In the epistles to pray in the spirit is to pray or speak in tongues. **1 Corinthians 14:14**; *"For if I pray in an unknown tongue, **my spirit** prayeth, but my understanding is unfruitful"*. **1 Corinthians 14:2**; *"For he that* *speaketh in an unknown tongue speaketh not unto men, but unto God: for no man understandeth him; howbeit **in the spirit** he speaketh mysteries"* (KJV). Paul's lifestyle of prayer was in tongues. **1 Corinthians 14:18**; *"I thank my God, I speak with tongues more than ye all:"* Every believer can pray in tongues; **Mark 16:17**; *"And these signs shall follow **them that believe**; In my name shall they cast out devils; they shall **speak with new tongues**"* (KJV). Thus, you see again, it is a prayer to God, not to man **(1 Corinthians 14:2).**

God is a spirit being, hence, the instruction to pray always in the spirit (in tongues). Praying in tongues is not productive and of no benefit to others listening or hearing the one praying in the spirit. Jude also instructed us to pray in the Holy Ghost. **Jude 1:20**; *"But ye, beloved, building up yourselves on your most holy faith, **praying in the Holy Ghost**"* (KJV). When you pray in tongues, you edify or build yourself up. Therefore, praying in tongues changes circumstances and meet the needs of others or fellow believers. It also edifies the one praying. You ought to ensure you pray in the spirit always as a lifestyle and not occasionally.

Knowing how to pray does not take the place of praying itself. In **Luke 11:1**; *"And it came to pass, that, as he was praying in a certain place, when he ceased, one of his disciples said unto him, Lord, teach us to pray, as John also taught his* *disciples"* (KJV). It is essential to note that there is an actual act of praying. You pray either according to precepts by teaching or according to example by show of action. This act of praying means there is a difference in knowing what prayer is and or what it entails.

Jesus taught his disciples how to pray and showed them how to pray by his example. *Prayer is an art.* Thus, the essence of being taught how to pray is for worship to be done the right way. Learning how to pray does not replace praying itself. The believer ought to be taught the art of prayer, for the believer to pray effectively. Hence it is vital to observe men from the scriptures and learn from them.

The example of Abraham in **Genesis 19:27**; *"And Abraham gat up early in the morning to the place where he stood before the **Lord**"* (KJV). The heart of David was aflame with a passionate zeal for his Lord. Observe the cry of David's heart in **Psalm 63:1**; *"O God, thou art my God; early will I seek thee: my soul thirsteth for thee, my flesh longeth for thee in a dry and thirsty land, where no water is;"* (KJV). Elijah was a man that prays **1 Kings 18:41–44.**

James 5:17-18; *"**17.** Elias was a man subject to like passions as we are, and he prayed earnestly that it might not rain: and it rained not on the earth by the space of **three years and six***

months. **18.** *"And he prayed again, and the heaven gave rain, and the earth brought forth her fruit"* (KJV). Jesus' life was characterized by earnest devotion to His Father. **Mark 1:35**; *"And in the morning, rising up a great while before day, he went out, and departed into a solitary place, and there prayed".* **Luke 3:21**; *"Now when all the people were baptized, it came to pass, that Jesus also being baptized, and praying, the heaven was opened,"* (KJV).

Jesus is God that became a man, yet He could not do without prayer. **John 1:1, 14**; *"1. In the beginning was the Word, and the Word was with God, and the Word was God. 14. And the Word was made flesh, and dwelt among us, (and we beheld his glory, the glory as of the only begotten of the Father,) full of grace and truth"* (KJV). Jesus is God manifest in the flesh, and the prophets prophesied of His humanity in **Isaiah 7:14**. The word Immanuel means *'God is with us'.* This was fulfilled in Jesus. Apostle Paul in **1 Timothy 3:16** also wrote of him saying; *"And without controversy great is the mystery of godliness: God was manifest in the flesh, justified in the Spirit, seen of angels, preached unto the Gentiles, believed on in the world, received up into glory".*

Jesus is one man that should have done without prayer, but his examples showed otherwise. According to the book of **Isaiah 7:14** and **1**

Timothy 3:16, we can see that in essence, God was manifest in the flesh in the person of Jesus Christ, which is why Paul taught that Jesus took upon himself the nature of man. Thus, Jesus is God that became a man; yet he prayed. The synoptic gospels give the record of his prayer life. **Luke 5:16**; *"And he withdrew himself into the wilderness, and prayed"* (KJV).

There were times when Jesus separated himself from people to pray. He also woke up early in the morning before the day to pray. **Matthew 14:23**; *"And when he had sent the multitudes away, he went up into a mountain apart to pray: and when the evening was come, he was there alone"* (KJV). Jesus departed to the mountain to pray. He also prayed all night. **Luke 6:12**; *"And it came to pass in those days, that he went out into a mountain to pray, and continued **all night in prayer** to God"* (KJV).

John 17:1, 9, 20; *"**1.** These words spake Jesus, and lifted up his eyes to heaven, and said, Father, the hour is come; glorify thy Son, that thy Son also may glorify thee: **9.** I pray for them: I pray not for the world, but for them which thou hast given me; for they are thine. **20.** Neither pray I for these alone, but for them also which shall believe on me through their word;"* (KJV). **Mark 14:32, 35, 39**; *"And they came to a place which was named Gethsemane: and he saith to his disciples, Sit ye* *here, while I shall pray.* **35.** *And he went forward a little, and fell on the ground, and prayed that, if it were possible, the hour might pass from him.* **39.** *And again he went away, and prayed, and spake the same words"* (KJV).

Matthew 26:39, 42, 44; *"39. And he went a little further, and fell on his face, and prayed, saying, O my Father, if it be possible, let this cup pass from me: nevertheless not as I will, but as thou wilt.* **42.** *He went away again the second time, and prayed, saying, O my Father, if this cup may not pass away from me, except I drink it, thy will be done.* **44.** *And he left them, and went away again, and prayed the third time, saying the same words* (KJV). **Luke 22:41–44**; *"41. And he was withdrawn from them about a stone's cast, and kneeled down, and prayed,* **42.** *Saying, Father, if thou be willing, remove this cup from me: nevertheless not my will, but thine, be done.* **43.** *And there appeared an angel unto him from heaven, strengthening him.* **44.** *And being in an agony he prayed more earnestly: and his sweat was as it were great drops of blood falling down to the ground"* (KJV).

Jesus is your perfect example. He took deliberate steps to pray and did not mutter the prayer in his mind but speak them out. Jesus had a lifestyle of worship. Jesus had a lifestyle of prayer. Recall that Jesus is God who became man, anointed of the Holy Ghost, yet you can see that prayer was a vital part of his life and ministry. Hence, it is evident that prayer is essential in the life and ministry of every man born of God's spirit. **Acts 10:38**; *"How God **anointed Jesus** of Nazareth with the Holy Ghost and with power: who went about doing good and healing all that were oppressed of the devil; for God was with him"* (KJV).

The disciples devoted themselves to prayer. Their devotion to the Lord was what made them devoted to prayer. For them, prayer was a means of closely walking with the Lord; it was not for material gain or for the miracles they needed. No special committee or prayer contractors were employed. Instead, each of these disciples indeed continued in prayer with one accord. The Holy Ghost came down mightily upon the disciples of old due to their selfless devotion and commitment to prayer. Disciples multiplied, and God wrought great wonders among them.

Act 1:13, 14; *"***13.** *And when they were come in, they went up into an upper room, where abode both Peter, and James, and John, and Andrew, Philip, and Thomas, Bartholomew, and Matthew, James the son of Alphaeus, and Simon Zelotes, and Judas the brother of James.* **14.** *These all continued with **one accord in prayer** and supplication, with the women, and Mary the mother of Jesus, and with his brethren"* (KJV).

Act 2:1–4; *"1. And when the day of Pentecost was fully come, they were all with **one accord** in one place. 2. And suddenly there came a sound from heaven as of a rushing mighty wind, and it filled all the house where they were sitting. 3. And there appeared unto them cloven tongues like as of fire, and it sat upon each of them. 4. And **they were all filled with the Holy Ghost**, and began to speak with other tongues, as the Spirit gave them utterance"* (KJV).

Act 2:41–43; *"41. Then they that gladly received his word were baptized: and the same day there were added unto them about three thousand souls. 42. And they continued stedfastly in the apostles' doctrine and fellowship, and in breaking of bread, and in prayers. 43. And fear came upon every soul: and many wonders and signs were done by the apostles"* (KJV).   The truth is that if you desire to experience God as these men and women did in the **Acts of the Apostles**, your devotion to prayer cannot be less than theirs. You must also be selfless in your commitment to prayer.

Examples from the Church in the Epistles

The church was also given to prayer. Prayer was something they attended regularly. The church was diligent, consistent, and they persevered in the place of prayer. **Act 1:14**; *"These all continued with one accord in prayer and supplication, with the* *women, and Mary the mother of Jesus, and with his brethren".* **Act 2:42**; *"And they continued stedfastly in the apostles' doctrine and fellowship, and in breaking of bread, and in prayers"* (KJV). The early church art of continuous prayer shows that the church has remained diligent in prayer and consistent with the lifestyle of worship.

Act 4:31; *"And when **they had prayed**, the place was shaken where they were assembled together; and they were all filled with the Holy Ghost, and they spake the word of God with boldness".* This group of believers in the **Acts of the Apostles** knew that prayer makes power available; hence they put it into action. They prayed, and the result was boldness, and more people were saved. When a church does not practice prayer consistently, it shows that they do not trust God's power at work in the church. **Act 12:5**; *"Peter therefore was kept in prison: but **prayer was made without ceasing of the church** unto God for him"* (KJV). The church prayed without ceasing for Peter's deliverance. **Acts 6:6**; *"Whom they set before the apostles: and when they had prayed, they laid their hands on them"* (KJV). In the local church, you see that prayer was a necessary and vital part of Christian activity in the church.

Paul was engaged in fasting and prayer with the church. **Act 14:21–23**; *"21. And when they had preached the gospel to that city, and had taught* *many, they returned again to Lystra, and to Iconium, and Antioch,.* **22.** *Confirming the souls of the disciples, and exhorting them to continue in the faith, and that we must through much tribulation enter into the kingdom of God.* **23.** *And when they had ordained them elders in every church, and had* **prayed with fasting***, they commended them to the Lord, on whom they believed"* (KJV). Even though it is good to fast, a believer does not necessarily need to fast to receive anything from God. It is not because you fasted that your prayers are answered. With or without fasting, God still answers prayers.

Fasting brings consecration; a separation from every distraction while you commune with God. The New Testament fasting is not to receive but for you to create time to pray, study, know what Christ has done for you, and to be equipped spiritually. The disciples were willing to forego food to concentrate on prayer. It was a further sign of their commitment to worship (prayer) in their walk with the Lord. **Act 13:2, 3**; *"2. As they ministered to the Lord, and fasted, the Holy Ghost said, Separate me Barnabas and Saul for the work whereunto I have called them.* **3.** *And when they had* **fasted and prayed***, and laid their hands on them, they sent them away".* **Act 14:23**; *"And when they had ordained them elders in every church, and had* **prayed with fasting***, they commended them to the Lord, on whom they believed"* (KJV).

Matthew 9:14; *"Then came to him the disciples of John, saying, Why do we and the Pharisees fast oft, but thy disciples fast not?* **15.** *And Jesus said unto them, Can the children of the bridechamber mourn, as long as the bridegroom is with them? But the days will come, when the bridegroom shall be taken from them, and then shall they fast"* (KJV). Now that you have access to the father by the blood of Jesus, *fasting is meant to help you downplay your appetite and put your body under control.* It helps you to connect more easily with God, to let the power of God flow through you to lose the bonds of wickedness, undo heavy burdens, let the oppressed go free, and do other great works in the name of the Lord and to the glory of God.

Laziness in prayer and fasting is also a strong indication of a lack of commitment to the Lord. Jesus subjected himself to fasting and prayers to show you how to live and walk with God as human beings. Thus, if Jesus devoted himself to prayer and sometimes with fasting, you should follow in His steps. That said, when Paul and Silas were in prison, instead of complaining, they engaged in prayer. **Act 16:23–25**; *"23. And when they had laid many stripes upon them, they cast them into prison, charging the jailor to keep them safely:* **24.** *Who, having received such a charge, thrust them into the inner prison, and made their feet fast in the stocks.* **25.** *And at midnight*

Paul and Silas prayed, and sang praises unto God: and the prisoners heard them" (KJV).

Prayer was a culture that was practiced throughout the **Acts of the Apostles,** as you can see. Prayer is a constant. It has no season; it is done in and out of season; that means its season is ***continuous***. Prayer has no time or place to be put into practice. Believers must be given to always praying either individually or collectively as a church. There is never a specific time that prayer is not essential. The church did not just teach the subject of prayer but also practiced it, **praying continuously**. Hence a believer should always pray. It will be seen as living in disobedience when one is not living a consistent lifestyle of prayer. It also indicates a Christian who refuses to make use of God's given authority.

Prayer of Faith

James 1:5–8; *"5. If any of you lack wisdom, let him ask of God, that giveth to all men liberally, and upbraideth not; and it shall be given him. 6. But let him ask in faith, nothing wavering. For he that wavereth is like a wave of the sea driven with the wind and tossed. 7. For let not that man think that he shall receive anything of the Lord. 8. A double minded man is unstable in all his ways"* (KJV).

James 1:5–8 shows that prayer goes beyond making requests unto God. It also involves receiving from God. In other words, receiving is part of prayer. Brother James made it clear why the believer who asked will not receive... *"But **let him ask in faith, nothing wavering**"*. He explains 'wavering' as being double minded in **verse 8**. The word 'wavering' implies to judge; to separate thoroughly between two things or opinions; to dispute. Wavering in this context means it can either be positive or negative, often used for deciding between two things.

In **James 2:4** it says; *"Are ye not then partial in yourselves and are become judges of evil thoughts?"* (KJV). In essence, James explains the term 'wavering' as an act of unbelief. So, in the place of prayer, the believer's opinion about God is crucial. In **James 1:6**; *"But let him ask in faith, nothing wavering. For he that wavereth is like a wave of the sea driven with the wind and tossed"* (KJV). The word asks in faith can be best understood as receiving in faith. It is faith demonstrated in God's character to give without finding fault.

The Bible says that the just shall live by faith **(Habakkuk 2:4; Romans 1:17; Galatians 3:11; Hebrews 10:38)**. It also says, *"... faith comes by hearing by the word of God"* **(Romans 10:17)**. Many Christians do not want to read, study, or meditate on God's word for themselves; neither do they want to pray for themselves. They do not wish to submit to the 'hearing of faith'. They want someone else to exercise the hearing of faith on their behalf. When believers are spiritual babies, it is easy to carry them with your faith. Spiritually speaking, every believer is called to grow and stand on their feet. God wants believers to enjoy a solitary walk with Him and receive God's blessings for themselves. It is not wrong for believers to ask someone else to intercede on their behalf. But if a believer never learned to seek God's face independently, such believers will never know the joy of trusting God personally. Consequently, they become unprepared to *'fight the good fight of faith'* when confronted with the' giant' challenges or test of life. Courage comes from having faith and a strong belief in God and His righteousness, even in hard times.

Remember, **John 8:32** says; *"And ye shall know the truth, and the truth shall make you free"* (KJV). In other words, it is not just the truth that makes you free; it is the truth that you know that makes you free. In other words, it is the truth that you know personally that makes you truly free. The truth that someone else knows may help or inspire you. But if you do not study that truth and learn it for yourself, you will find yourself at a disadvantage in life. You will only be able to defeat the giants in your life with prayer and what you know about God and His word.

Defeating the giants in your life is why it is vital to read, study and meditate on God's word until it becomes a part of you (in your spirit and not just in your head). In **Proverbs 16:18** it says, *"Pride goeth before destruction, and a haughty spirit before a fall"* (KJV). If you are not careful, you can begin to think that you are so special when it comes to spiritual battles. You can forget that Jesus is the one who stormed hell's gate and defeated the enemy once and for all through His death, burial, and resurrection.

All that remains for you (a believer) is to stand your ground in faith based on Christ's finished work. And you must remember that as you do, your present battles are the Lord's. Therefore, you receive victory in Christ Jesus. When you are walking with God, your faith and confidence in God will be tested. The enemy will challenge you to see if you believe what you say you hold onto (your belief). With God's word in your heart and on your lips, you can face the trials, poverty, sickness, disease, and life challenges in the place of prayer.

Why Would A Believer Not Receive?

A double-minded believer will not receive from God because of the lack of knowledge about God's character, which then affects requests in the place of prayer. **James 1:8**; *"A double minded man* *is unstable in all his ways"* (KJV). Understanding God's character around prayer is fundamental. The first thing a believer must understand in the walk with God is the character of Him. In James's writings, he described *Him as the giving God who does not find fault,* meaning there is no refusal in God's character. In prayer, you are fellowshipping with the Father and the Son (Jesus). **1 John 1:3**; *"That which we have seen and heard declare we unto you, that ye also may have fellowship with us: and truly **our fellowship is with the Father, and with his Son Jesus Christ**"* (KJV).

The focus of Jesus' teaching on prayer was on knowing the Father. That means prayer is not primarily about the things or the results you get but Fellowship with the Father. **Matthew 6:9**; *"After this manner therefore pray ye: **Our Father** which art in heaven, Hallowed be thy name".* **Matthew 7:11**; *"If ye then, being evil, know how to give good gifts unto your children, how much more shall **your Father** which is in heaven give good things to them that ask him?"* (KJV). Jesus always spoke about the Father in the place of prayer. Therefore, when praying, the consciousness of the Father is critical.

Jesus always spoke about the Father in the place of prayer. Therefore, when praying, the consciousness of the Father is critical. In teaching prayer, the emphasis is on the Father. You have fellowship with the Father in prayer, and you should not lose focus of that. In Jesus' prayer life, you see a consistent emphasis on the Father's person in the way he prayed. **John 17:1**; *"These words spake Jesus, and lifted up his eyes to heaven, and said, **Father**, the hour is come; glorify thy Son, that thy Son also may glorify thee:"* (KJV).

John 11:41; *"Then they took away the stone from the place where the dead was laid. And Jesus lifted up his eyes, and said, **Father**, I thank thee that thou hast heard me".* **John 16:23, 24**; *"**23.** And in that day ye shall ask me nothing. Verily, verily, I say unto you, Whatsoever ye shall ask the **Father** in my name, he will give it you. **24.** Hitherto have ye asked nothing in my name: ask, and ye shall receive, that your joy may be full"* (KJV).

In the epistles, the word 'Father' was also mentioned. **Act 2:33**; *"Therefore being by the right hand of God exalted, and having received of the **Father** the promise of the Holy Ghost, he hath shed forth this, which ye now see and hear".* **1 Thessalonians 1:1–3**; *"**1.** Paul, and Silvanus, and Timotheus, unto the church of the Thessalonians which is in **God the Father** and in the Lord Jesus Christ: Grace be unto you, and peace, from **God our Father**, and the Lord Jesus Christ. **2.** We give thanks to God always for you all, making mention of you in **our prayers**; **3.** Remembering without ceasing your work of faith, and labour of love, and patience of hope in our Lord Jesus Christ, in the sight of **God*** *and our Father"* (KJV). **1 Timothy 1:2**; *"Unto Timothy, my own son in the faith: Grace, mercy, and peace, from* **God our Father** *and Jesus Christ our Lord"* (KJV).

Observe the use of the word 'Father' in the above scriptures. It speaks of paternity. Hence, your fellowship with the Father in prayer. Because He abides in you, you do not go to God in the place of prayer but rather fellowship with him. Calling God, a Father in prayer, affirms your union with Him in Christ. Thus, prayer is taking your place in Christ over life's circumstances.

Reason for A Believer to Waver (Doubt) in Prayer

In **James 1:5–7**; the focus is on the character of God. Thus, the wavering is about the nature of God. Let us examine how the nature of God was described; *He gives to all men liberally without finding faults.* Here you see God as a giving God, who does not find guilt or blame before He gives. *He does not tempt with evil,* meaning *He is without variableness or shadow of turning* **(James 1:17).** He does not change, and He is your Father. Therefore, it is paramount that when you pray, your focus should be on the Father and you can receive.

Every time the believer prays to the Father, He hears and gives. Giving is consistent with God's nature. **James 1:17**; *"Every good gift and every perfect gift is from above, and cometh down from the Father of lights, with whom is no variableness, neither shadow of turning"* (KJV). Thus, receiving after praying is dependent solely on the one asking and not God. You are responsible for receiving what you asked because God gives every time you ask. The focus is on the believer receiving, and not God giving. *"**Let him ask in faith** ... "* James's emphasis is on the believer wavering in his mind about the character of God in giving. A wavering mindset hinders the believer from receiving answers released by God in response to offered prayers.

Prayer makes power available. In... **James 5:16**; *"Confess your faults one to another, and pray one for another, that ye may be healed. The effectual fervent prayer of a righteous man availeth much"* (KJV). Consequently, in the place of prayer, power is made available to meet the need and to change circumstances. James mentioned that the prayer of a righteous man makes power possible. *The believer is the upright (righteous) man* because the believer has been made righteous by his identification with Christ. **2. Corinthians 5:21;** *"For he hath made him to be sin for us, who knew no sin; that we might be made the righteousness of God in him"* (KJV).

The believer has been made the righteousness of God in Him (Christ). Thus, the righteous man can pray without fault or doubt. **James 5:14**; *"14. Is any sick among you? Let him call for the elders of the church; and let them pray over him, anointing him with oil in the name of the Lord:* **15.** *And the prayer of faith shall save the sick, and the Lord shall raise him up; and if he have committed sins, they shall be forgiven him.* *"*(KJV).... ***the prayer of faith****…"* Praying without fault or doubt, which is the prayer of faith, helps you to see that when you ask in prayer, it is in God's character to be consistent in giving whatsoever you ask by His will.

Therefore, exercising faith in praying has to do with receiving, which is dependent on the part of the one asking (believer) and not the one giving (God). Faith is not required in asking but in receiving because you do not need faith to communicate with the Father, as explained in **James 1:5**. Brother James taught that, *"If any of you lack wisdom, let him ask of God, that giveth to all men liberally, and upbraideth not; and it shall be given him"* (KJV). There are no qualifications for God to give. All it takes is the mouth to request without wavering. God is not looking for a condition for why He should give because He gives to all men liberally. **John 6:35**; *"And Jesus said unto them, I am the bread of life: he that cometh to me shall never hunger; and he that believeth on me shall never thirst"* (KJV).

The responsibility of the believer (asker) to receive what the father has given is by believing. Believing demonstrates the believer's (the recipient) willingness to accept what God has given in His son Jesus. Hence when a man chooses not to receive (what God has given), it does not change the fact that God has already given. It also does not change God's character as one who gives all men freely without finding fault. God's responsibility, which was demonstrated by his nature of love, was to give his son.

Your responsibility is to receive by believing; in… **John 3:16**; *"For God so loved the world, that he gave his only begotten Son, that whosoever* **believeth** *in him should not perish, but have everlasting life"* (KJV). Everlasting life is only received when a man believes. Thus, receiving is an activity that occurs consciously. Hence you must accept in prayer when you ask consciously. The day a man believes and receives, is not the day God gave or answered his prayer. The recipient has only taken advantage of what has already been given in Christ.

Thus, a man consciously receives in prayer as an act of the man's will and choose not to be passive but want to receive in prayer by speaking his expectations actively. Hope is part of a believer's life. God places hope (life of expectation) in you. In Christ, you have been given an expectation. Hence, hope is part of the life of faith. **1 Corinthians 13:13**; *And now abideth faith, hope, charity, these three; but the greatest of these is charity* (KJV). Hope is not about having positive thinking, but an earnest expectation of results based on God's word. The term 'hope' must be well understood in opinion and in praying the prayer of faith. If you make a request from your mouth and do not doubt, you will have what you say.

Mark 11:23, 24; *"***23.** *For verily I say unto you, That whosoever shall say unto this mountain, Be thou removed, and be thou cast into the sea; and shall not doubt in his heart, but shall BELIEVE that those things which he saith shall come to pass; he shall have whatsoever he SAITH.* **24.** *Therefore I say unto you, What things so ever ye desire, when ye pray, believe that ye receive them, and ye shall have them* (KJV). That means when praying, you must expect to receive answers. **"What things so ever ye desire, when ye pray, believe that ye receive them, and ye shall have them"** is the prayer of faith.

Note that it is possible to pray without expectation. If prayer automatically means hope, then Jesus will not mention expectation, which becomes necessary in receiving answers to prayer. *"Believe that ye receive them, and ye shall have them",* you will have whatsoever you desire when you pray. From the Bible verse above, receiving is when you pray, while having what you asked for is afterward. Thus, the prayer of faith means accepting in worship (prayer). **Ephesians 2:8**; *"For by grace are ye saved through faith; and that not of yourselves: it is the gift of God:"* (KJV). **2 Corinthians 4:13**; *"We having the same spirit of faith, according as it is written, **I believed**, and therefore have **I spoken**; we also believe, and therefore **speak**;"*. You can see from 2 Corinthians 4:13 that this is the same spirit of faith that Jesus talked about in Mark 11:23.

A believer is not someone who lacks faith or has a problem of believing. A man without Christ has a believing problem and does not have faith. As a believer, you pray in tongues, which is praying in the spirit. When you are praying in the spirit, you are praying the will of God. So, you should focus on who God is – He is your Father, who gives freely and does not fault. You should make it an act to focus your gaze on the giving God in the place of prayer.

Do not Pray for Faith

You do not ask for faith because every believer has a measure of the God kind of faith. In **Mark 11: 22–24**; *"**22**. And Jesus answering saith unto them, Have faith in God. **23**. For verily I say unto you, That whosoever shall say unto this* *mountain, Be thou removed, and be thou cast into the sea; and shall not doubt in his heart, but shall believe that those things which he saith shall come to pass; he shall have whatsoever he saith.* **24.** *Therefore I say unto you, What things so ever ye desire, when ye pray, believe that ye receive them, and ye shall have them"* (KJV). You can see in verse 22, Jesus said to them, have faith in God, translated by the Greek scholars to means "have the God-kind of faith." So, in other words, Jesus was saying to them literally, "have the God-kind of faith."

In **Mark 11:11–14, 20–22**; *"11. Jesus had just demonstrated to the disciples that He had that Kind of faith (the God kind of faith).* *"12. And on the morrow, when they were come from Bethany, he was hungry:* **13.** *And seeing a fig tree afar off having leaves, he came, if haply he might find anything thereon: and when he came to it, he found nothing but leaves; for the time of figs was not yet.* **14.** *And Jesus answered and said unto it, No man eat fruit of thee hereafter forever. And his disciples heard it.* **20.** *And in the morning, as they passed by, they saw the fig tree dried up from the roots.* **21.** *And Peter calling to remembrance saith unto him, Master, behold, the fig tree which thou cursedst is withered away.* **22.** *And Jesus answering saith unto them, Have faith in God* (KJV).

God's kind of faith is the type you believe in your heart, and then confess with your mouth what you believe in your heart. This kind of faith is the same type of faith God used to create the world. God believed that what He said would come to pass, "He said, let there be light, and there was light." Hence, God created the sun, moon, stars, animals by speaking them into existence and believing that what He said would come to pass, and indeed it came to pass. All of God's creation (except man) came into existence because God spoke them into being. That is the God kind of faith. In Mark 11:11–14, 20–22, Jesus said to His disciples, "you have the God kind of faith." So, it will be a waste of time to be asking for faith in prayer because every believer already has a measure of the God kind of faith. You do not have to get it, pray for it, fast for it, and you do not have to promise to be of good behavior to get it. You already have it.

Romans 12:3; "*For I say, through the grace given unto me, **to every man that is among you**, not to think of himself more highly than he ought to think; but to think soberly, according as **God hath dealt to every man the measure of faith** (KJV)*". … **to every man that is among you***… Paul was referring to the believers. As a believer, when you are faced with life's challenges, you don't say, "I don't have faith," because it means you were not a believer in the first instance, so you need to get saved. You need to be saved because unsaved people do not have faith, and saved people indeed have faith. You cannot be saved if you do not have faith – *"... faith cometh by hearing, and hearing by the word of God"*. **Ephesians 2:8**; *For by grace are ye saved through faith; and that not of yourselves: it is the gift of God:* **Romans 10:17**; *So then faith cometh by hearing, and hearing by the word of God* (KJV).

The word of God is the word of faith because God's word builds faith. God's word causes faith to come to the heart of those who are open to it. **Romans 10:8**; *But what saith it? The word is nigh thee, even in thy mouth, and in thy heart: that is, the WORD of FAITH, which we preach*; (KJV). Unless a believer recognizes or realizes they already have faith, the problem or statement of 'I don't have faith' will not be solved, and it will keep arising. Unfortunately, some believers have this knowledge, but they do not put it to work when confronted with life issues. It is essential to know that all believers have faith, according to the Bible. Kenneth E. Hagins said, *"if what you hear preached – doesn't cause faith to come and build faith in your spirit, then it either isn't the Word of God or else you are not hearing it"*. The Bible says, *"... faith cometh by hearing, and hearing by the word of God"*. Hence whenever you pray, do not doubt, do not murmur, nor grumble. Exercise your God kind of faith, and it will unfailingly yield results.

How Do We Receive in Prayer?

1 Timothy 2:1; *"I exhort therefore, that, first of all, supplications, prayers, intercessions, and **giving of thanks**, be made for all men"* (KJV). It is important to note that in prayer, giving thanks comes after the request has been made. Thanksgiving after prayer shows that you believe you have received what you requested from God. **1 John 5:14-15**; *"**14.** And this is the confidence that we have in him, that, if we ask any thing according to his will, he heareth us: **15.** And if we know that he hear us, whatsoever we ask, we know that we have the petitions that we desired of him"* (KJV).

You need to understand that the Father always hears you when you pray. The knowing is about God's character, which is why He always hears you when you pray. As a child of God almighty, you have answers in prayer, and you should choose to renew your mind about God's character continually. As a believer, you should know how to act on your receiving. Jesus' teaching on prayer in Mark 11:24 clearly shows that receiving is when you pray while having your requests is afterward. Receiving in prayer is the prayer of faith.

Hence the vital issue is knowledge, knowing that the Father always hears you when you pray. **James 1:5**; *If any of you lack wisdom, let him ask of*

God, that giveth to all men liberally, and upbraideth not; and it shall be given him. **6.** *But let him ask in faith, nothing wavering. For he that wavereth is like a wave of the sea driven with the wind and tossed.* **7.** *For let not that man think that he shall receive any thing of the Lord* (KJV). **1 John 5:15**; *And if we know that **he hear us**, whatsoever we ask, we know that we have the petitions that we desired of him* (KJV). Based on the scriptures, Jesus Christ, Apostle Paul, and the men of old all prayed. In praying, they were not imagining or guessing or wishing that they would receive prayer answers. They were not doubtful, and they had the belief that God hears, and He indeed heard them. And since God's character is consistent, you should not forget that He always hears you when you pray.

Praying for Others

Ephesians 6:18; *Praying always with all prayer and supplication in the Spirit, and watching thereunto with all perseverance and supplication for all saints;* (KJV). The apostles concentrated more on praying for others than themselves. Some of the categories of people to pray for include.

Praying for the Unsaved

You are to pray for the unsaved. The unsaved is the one who has not believed or heard the gospel of Christ to the believer. **2 Corinthians 4:3**; *"But if our gospel be hid, it is hid to them that are lost"*. The unsaved person's mind is blinded and needs the light in the gospel of Christ, which can only happen when such a person hears the gospel of Jesus Christ. **Romans 10:14**; *"How then shall they call on him in whom they have not believed? And how shall they believe in him of whom they have not heard? And how shall they hear without a preacher?"* (KJV). The gospel must be preached for such a person to listen to and then to believe, hence the individual needs a preacher.

Romans 10:15; *"And how shall they preach, except they be sent? As it is written, How beautiful are the feet of them that preach the gospel of peace, and bring glad tidings of good things?"* In praying for the unsaved, pray for someone to reach the unsaved (that is where you can't directly contact the unsaved person). **Matthew 9:37**; *"Then saith he unto his disciples, The harvest truly is plenteous, but the laborers are few;* (KJV). Pray for a free flow of the gospel to the hearing of the unsaved, and that the word has a free course and is glorified". **2 Thessalonians 3:1**; *"Finally, brethren, pray for us, that the word of the Lord may have free course, and be glorified, even as it is with you"* (KJV). Pray for boldness of the preacher sent to the unsaved person.

An example of how the gospel was preached to the unsaved is seen in **Acts 10:1–45**; *"***1.** *There was a certain man in Caesarea called Cornelius, a centurion of the band called the Italian band,.* **2.** *A devout man, and one that feared God with all his house, which gave much alms to the people, and prayed to God always.* **3.** *He saw in a vision evidently about the ninth hour of the day an angel of God coming in to him, and saying unto him, Cornelius.* **4.** *And when he looked on him, he was afraid, and said, What is it, Lord? And he said unto him, Thy prayers and thine alms are come up for a memorial before God.* **5.** *And now send men to Joppa, and call for one Simon, whose surname is Peter:* **6.** *He lodgeth with one Simon a tanner, whose house is by the sea side: he shall tell thee what thou oughtest to do.* **7.** *And when the angel which spake unto Cornelius was departed, he called two of his household servants, and a devout soldier of them that waited on him continually;* **8.** *And when he had declared all these things unto them, he sent them to Joppa.* **21.** *Then Peter went down to the men which were sent unto him from Cornelius; and said, Behold, I am he whom ye seek: what is the cause wherefore ye are come?* **22.** *And they said, Cornelius the centurion, a just man, and one that feareth God, and of good report among all the nation of the Jews, was warned from God by an holy angel to send for thee into his house, and to* *hear words of thee.* **23.** *Then called he them in, and lodged them. And on the morrow Peter went away with them, and certain brethren from Joppa accompanied him.* **24.** *And the morrow after they entered into Caesarea. And Cornelius waited for them and had called together his kinsmen and near friends.* **34.** *Then Peter opened his mouth, and said, Of a truth I perceive that God is no respecter of persons:* **35.** *But in every nation he that feareth him, and worketh righteousness, is accepted with him.* **44.** *While Peter yet spake these words, the Holy Ghost fell on all them which heard the word.* **45.** *And they of the circumcision which believed were astonished, as many as came with Peter, because that on the Gentiles also was poured out the gift of the Holy Ghost"* (KJV). You can see that Peter had to preach to Cornelius before he got saved. Despite Cornelius prayed and gave alms that did not get him saved. A preacher was needed.

Praying for Fellow Believers

After receiving salvation, what you need the most is the knowledge of the word of God to grow. **1 Peter 2:2**; *"As newborn babes, desire the sincere milk of the word, that ye may grow thereby"* (KJV). **1 Peter 3:18**; *"For Christ also hath once suffered for sins, the just for the unjust, that he might bring us to God, being put to death in the flesh, but quickened* *by the Spirit"* (KJV). The growth is in the knowledge of your salvation, and you can see this consistently in Paul's prayer for the churches.

Ephesians 1:16-23; *"***16.** *Cease not to give thanks for you, making mention of you in my prayers;* **17.** *That the God of our Lord Jesus Christ, the Father of glory, may give unto you the spirit of wisdom and revelation in the knowledge of him:* **18.** *The eyes of your understanding being enlightened; that ye may know what is the hope of his calling, and what the riches of the glory of his inheritance in the saints,* **19.** *And what is the exceeding greatness of his power to us-ward who believe, according to the working of his mighty power,* **20.** *Which he wrought in Christ, when he raised him from the dead, and set him at his own right hand in the heavenly places,* **21.** *Far above all principality, and power, and might, and dominion, and every name that is named, not only in this world, but also in that which is to come:* **22.** *And hath put all things under his feet, and gave him to be the head over all things to the church,* **23.** *Which is his body, the abored of him that filleth all in all"* (KJV).

Praying for insights for fellow believers should not be for power because Ephesians 19 already laid down that His power is at work towards everyone who believes. The believer needs revelation knowledge which is the reason why Paul consistently prayed for the believer to be full of knowledge because your fellowship becomes more effective only when you have a precise understanding of who you are and what you have in Christ Jesus. **Philippians 1:9–11**; *"9. And this I pray, that your love may abound yet more and more in knowledge and in all judgment; 10. That ye may approve things that are excellent; that ye may be sincere and without offence till the day of Christ; 11. Being filled with the fruits of righteousness, which are by Jesus Christ, unto the glory and praise of God"* (KJV).

Colossians 1:9–11; *"9. For this cause we also, since the day we heard it, do not cease to pray for you, and to desire that ye might be filled with the knowledge of his will in all wisdom and spiritual understanding; 10. That ye might walk worthy of the Lord unto all pleasing, being fruitful in every good work, and increasing in the knowledge of God; 11. Strengthened with all might, according to his glorious power, unto all patience and long suffering with joyfulness;"* (KJV). **Philemon 1:4**; *"I thank my God, making mention of thee always in my prayers,"* (KJV). Hence, it is paramount to pray for believers to grow in every good work, such that they walk in God's plan and purpose and be effective as Christians.

Praying for Ministers of the Gospel

The Apostles asked that you pray for them. This request to pray for the apostles implies that the ministers of God ought to be prayed for, particularly for the work of the ministry. **Ephesians 6:18–20**; *"***18.** Praying always with all prayer and supplication in the Spirit, and watching thereunto with all perseverance and supplication for all saints;* **19.** *And for me, that utterance may be given unto me, that I may open my mouth boldly, to make known the mystery of the gospel,* **20.** *For which I am an ambassador in bonds: that therein I may speak boldly, as I ought to speak"* (KJV).

Colossians 4:2–4; *"***2.** Continue in prayer, and watch in the same with thanksgiving;* **3.** *Withal praying also for us, that God would open unto us a door of utterance, to speak the mystery of Christ, for which I am also in bonds:* **4.** *That I may make it manifest, as I ought to speak"* (KJV). Praying always for all saints would include your ministers (pastors and leaders in the church). You are to pray for utterance and boldness to speak God's word as they ought to. **Act 4:29**; *"And now, Lord, behold their threatenings: and grant unto thy servants, that with all boldness they may speak thy word"* (KJV). You are to pray for the Gospel to be received without hindrances and for lives to be preserved – **Romans 15:3–31; 2 Thessalonians 3:1–2.**

In addition to praying for boldness, utterance, and the ministry to be received unhindered, you ought to *pray signs and wonders shall follow their ministries.* **Romans 15:19**; *"Through mighty signs and wonders, by the power of the Spirit of God; so that from Jerusalem, and round about unto Illyricum, I have fully preached the gospel of Christ"* (KJV). **Acts 4:30**; *"By stretching forth thine hand to heal; and that signs and wonders may be done by the name of thy holy child Jesus"* (KJV).

Pray for the ministers to remain honest and maintain conduct pleasing to God. **Hebrews 13:18**; *"Pray for us: for we trust we have a good conscience, in all things willing to live honestly"* (KJV). Pray for them to maintain their integrity in service. **1 Corinthians 16:9**; *"For a great door and effectual is opened unto me, and there are many adversaries"* (KJV). Pray for them to overcome opposition they faced in many areas of the ministry. Prayer is not just communication. Prayer is the breath of the regenerated spirit. It is having the correct approach to communicating with God because it takes praying a right to be heard. Prayer is not optional for the believer because it is one of your responsibilities. That is why the word of God admonishes that you pray always.

CHAPTER THREE

HARVEST/ RECEIVING IN PRAYER

MARK 11:24

"Therefore I say unto you, What things so ever ye desire, when ye pray, believe that ye receive them, and ye shall have them" (KJV).

Jesus made it clear that the one who has the responsibility to receive in the place of prayer is the one who is praying. Harvest in prayer involves you asking because when you do not ask, you do not receive it. That does not mean your heavenly Father is waiting until you ask before He gives you. At least you did not ask Him for life, sun, rain before He gave you, nor did you ask for forgiveness before He forgave you. All you did was to believe in Christ Jesus's finished work and accepted the forgiveness of sin. He has already given you all things in Christ Jesus, which you only need to receive. **1 John 5:14, 15**; *"***14.** *And this is the confidence that we have in him, that, if we ask anything according to his will, he heareth us:* **15.** *And if we know that he hear us, whatsoever we ask, we know that we have the petitions that we desired of him"* (KJV).

In prayer, you do not experience a delay from God. God always hears when you make a request. It is in His hearing that you are confident that He gives that which you asked. **James 1:5**; *"***5.** *If any of you lack wisdom, let him ask of God, that giveth to all men liberally, and upbraideth not; and it shall be given him.* **6.** *But let him ask in faith, nothing wavering. For he that wavereth is like a wave of the sea driven with the wind and tossed.* **7.** *For let not that man think that he shall receive anything of the Lord"* (KJV).

When asking, it should be in faith, same as what Jesus said, "**believe that you receive them**". God's character is to give to all without finding fault, which means it is your responsibility to accept what has been given. The receiving is by faith, a man who asks and doubts in his mind cannot receive from God. Asking without doubts to receive does not mean God has not given; instead, you have to receive/harvest by faith. In **Matthew 21:22**; Jesus said, *"And all things, whatsoever ye shall ask in prayer, believing, ye shall receive"* (KJV).

Hence, believing is key to receiving. When you ask, God gives, and you must accept. At salvation, God gave you Jesus, which you received by faith, believing in His resurrection. So also, you can only receive answers to your prayers by faith. Prayer goes beyond making requests unto God. It also involves receiving from God, making your ability to receive part and parcel of prayer. **James 1:5–8**; *"**5.** If any of you lack wisdom, let him ask of God, that giveth to all men liberally, and upbraideth not; and it shall be given him. **6.** But let him ask in faith, nothing wavering. For he that wavereth is like a wave of the sea driven with the wind and tossed. **7.** For let not that man think that he shall receive anything of the Lord. **8.** A double-minded man is unstable in all his ways"* (KJV).

The Epistle of James explained wavering to mean to be double-minded, which could either be positive or negative. Wavering is an act of unbelief. God is a giving God that gives to all men liberally without finding fault. He is without variableness or shadow of turning. God does not tempt with evil and is not responsible for situations that drive the believer to pray. God is your father that does not change. Hence, as a believer, you should do so without doubt or unbelief concerning whatsoever you ask of Him when you pray. **James 1:17**; *"Every good gift and every perfect gift is from above, and* *cometh down from the Father of lights, with whom is no variableness, neither shadow of turning"* (KJV).

In his writing, James explains that receiving after praying depends solely on the one asking and not God. God gives every time you ask. ***"But let him ask in faith…"*** In his writing, James explains that receiving after praying depends solely on the one asking and not God. God gives every time you ask. The focus and emphasis are on the believer (you) wavering in your mind about God's character in giving. This kind of mindset can hinder you from receiving/harvesting in prayer what God has given in response to your request.

In **James 5:16**, prayer makes power available. Thus, in the place of prayer, power is made available to meet your needs and change your circumstances. The prayer of a righteous man makes power available. *"Confess your faults one to another, and pray one for another, that ye may be healed. The effectual fervent **prayer of a righteous man availeth much.**"* (KJV). The believer is the righteous man. The believer has been made righteous by his identification with Jesus. **2 Corinthians 5:21**; *"For he hath made him to be sin for us, who knew no sin; that we might be made the righteousness of God in him"* (KJV).

The believer has been made the righteousness of God in Him (Christ). So, the righteous can pray without fault or doubt. In prayer, faith is not required in asking but in receiving, meaning faith is not needed to talk or get to God **(James 1:5)**. God is not looking for a condition of why He should give because He gives liberally. Giving freely to all men is the character of God, your Father. There is no qualification to be given anything from God. All it takes is for you to open your mouth and make a request. And when you do, do it without doubting or wavering. You need faith to receive/harvest and not to ask in prayer.

What to Do When Your Prayers Seem Unanswered

You must have had experiences where it looks like your prayer was not answered. But is that really what happened? The Bible says in **Matthew 7:7**; *"Ask, and it shall be given you; seek, and ye shall find; knock, and it shall be opened unto you."* (KJV). Is that true? Some People could cite examples where they did not receive after asking. You do not need to rely on others' experiences and testimonies who have prayed for something and never received from God, the Father.

You have got to make your decision based on **Romans 3:4**; where the Bible says, *"Let God be true, but every man [or in this case, every circumstance] a liar."* (KJV). God's Word is true, not your experiences. Overdependence on others' experiences is one of the reasons so much doctrinal division has come to be. The Word of God is manifest in its doctrine, but when someone tries the Word and doesn't see the promised results, rather than admit that they could have failed, they say something like, *"That must have passed away with the apostles"* or *"It must not have been God's will,"* etc.

God is not the one who failed to answer. Instead, you are the one who has been unable to receive what you requested. What happens when you ask in prayer is that God moves immediately and gives you the answer in your spirit. You are responsible for believing and acting accordingly to bring the answer to the physical world. God is a spirit (John 4:24), and He always supplies your answer (solution/needs) to your spirit man.

You are like a spiritual transformer that converts spiritual power to physical power just as radio signals are converted into frequencies audible to your ear. You do not hear the actual signal frequencies being broadcast by the radio station, but rather a signal that has been picked up by a receiver and translated into an audible sound. For a person to say that there are not any radio signals where they are, just because they cannot hear them, is not true. The signals are there, but they are on a higher frequency than the human ear can hear. They must be 'demodulated' into a lower frequency suitable for listening.

This analogy explains the way your answers to prayer come. God moves in the spirit world and gives you your answer by faith, and you convert it into a physical reality through your actions. That is not to say that you are the one who provided the answers to your prayer by your power. It is God who works the miracles, but they do come through you. Without Him, you can do nothing (John 15:5), but He has made you joint-heirs together with Christ so that He does nothing without you. **Ephesians 3:20**; says, *"Now unto him that is able to do exceeding abundantly above all that we ask or think, **according to the power that worketh in us**"*.

You have got a part to play in receiving from God. Ignorance of your role has been your most significant problem. Now you can understand much more clearly what **Mark 11:24** means by, *"What things so ever ye desire, when ye pray, believe that ye receive them, and ye shall have them."* (KJV). You receive in your spirit by faith immediately, and it shall come to pass in the physical later. It may be one minute, one day, or one year, but you cannot waiver in your belief that God has already answered your prayer. The time that it takes for God's answer to be manifest in the physical is dependent upon many things, but it is not God who determines that but you because *God answers immediately*.

Remember, it says you must believe that you receive *when you pray*. God is not asking you to believe something that is not true. You do receive instantly in your spirit, and then it is manifest in the physical later (see **Daniel 9 and 10)**. In chapter 9, Daniel prayed a prayer. While he was still praying, his answer to prayer came in the form of Angel Gabriel giving him *"skill and understanding"* in the thing he desired. That is a quick answer to prayer. However, in **verse 23**, Angel Gabriel says that God had sent him forth at the beginning of his prayer. God moved instantly, but it took some time for the answer to appear in the physical realm. In **Daniel chapter 10**, he prayed another prayer, and his response (answer) took three full weeks to manifest. What a difference!

Most people would say, *"I wonder why God answered that first prayer in a few minutes, and the second prayer took three weeks"*. But in **Daniel 10:12**, God answered the second prayer instantly too. Praise God! The Lord was not the variable in this case but a demonic force, ***"the prince of the kingdom of Persia,"*** that had hindered the answer to Daniel's prayer. Whether it be Satan or people's wills or unbelief or any of many other possible hindrances, you must know that it is not God who seems so unpredictable **(Psalm 102:27; Malachi 3:6)**.

Understanding that it is not God who seems unpredictable is a fundamental truth that you must establish before you can do anything about speeding up the answer to your prayer. If you have prayed a prayer in line with God's Word, God answers it immediately **(1 John 5:14, 15; Dan. 9, 10)**. If you understand that, you are ready to begin releasing your faith over bringing that answer into complete manifestation.

Harvesting answers in prayer has to do with your heart (believing) and your mouth (speaking), that is where power is made available in prayer harvest. God only supplies answers to the prayers that are in line with His character liked understanding He is a good God, and He does not kill **(James 1:16, 17)**. God is not part of any prayer to kill or destroy people's lives **(Luke 9:51, 56)**. You may pray those kinds of prayers and see results, but that does not mean God answered them but Satan. **John 10:10**; *"The thief cometh not, but for to steal, and to kill, and to destroy: I am come that they might have life, and that they might have it more abundantly"* (KJV). **John 8:44**; *Ye are of your father the devil, and the lusts of your father ye will do. He was a murderer from the beginning, and abode not in the truth, because there is no truth in him. When he speaketh a lie, he speaketh of his own: for he is a liar, and the father of it* (KJV).

You have God's given authority as a believer. You can allow God to use it and achieve good things or allow Satan/Demons to use it and achieve evil things. All these happen through your words expressed because your authority is expressed through spoken words. Be careful whom you allow using your authority. To know what God can do and what He cannot do, you should look at Jesus' life on earth, because He is God manifest **(John 5:19, 20; Colossians 1:15; Hebrews 1:3; Luke 9:51, 56)**. Jesus never kills, destroys, or gives people sickness. And that is what God does exactly. **Act 10:38**; *"How God anointed Jesus of Nazareth with the Holy Ghost and with power: who went about doing good, and **healing** all that were oppressed of the devil; for God was with him"* (KJV).

Knowledge is needed in trusting God for healing **Isaiah 53: 4-5;** *Surely he hath borne our griefs, and carried our sorrows: yet we did esteem him stricken, smitten of God, and afflicted. But he was wounded for our transgressions; he was bruised for our iniquities: the chastisement of our peace was upon him; and **with his stripes we are healed**.* So, healing is your heritage in Christ Jesus. Irrespective of the illness or diseases or ugly circumstances, you must exercise your authority.

CHAPTER FOUR
PRAYER FOR THOSE IN AUTHORITY
DANIEL 3:1–18

In **Daniel 3:1–18**, "**1.** *King Nebuchadnezzar made an image of gold, sixty cubits high and six cubits wide, and set it up on the plain of Dura in the province of Babylon.* **2.** *He then summoned the satraps, prefects, governors, advisers, treasurers, judges, magistrates and all the other provincial officials to come to the dedication of the image he had set up.* **3.** *So the satraps, prefects, governors, advisers, treasurers, judges, magistrates and all the other provincial officials assembled for the* *dedication of the image that King Nebuchadnezzar had set up, and they stood before it.* **4.** *Then the herald loudly proclaimed, 'Nations and peoples of every language, this is what you are commanded to do:* **5.** *As soon as you hear the sound of the horn, flute, zither, lyre, harp, pipe and all kinds of music, you must fall down and worship the image of gold that King Nebuchadnezzar has set up.* **6.** *Whoever does not fall down and worship will immediately be thrown into a blazing furnace.'* **7.** *Therefore, as soon as they heard the sound of the horn, flute, zither, lyre, harp and all kinds of music, all the nations and peoples of every language fell down and worshiped the image of gold that King Nebuchadnezzar had set up.* **8.** *At this time some astrologers came forward and denounced the Jews.* **9.** *They said to King Nebuchadnezzar, 'May the king live forever!* **10.** *Your Majesty has issued a decree that everyone who hears the sound of the horn, flute, zither, lyre, harp, pipe and all kinds of music must fall down and worship the image of gold,* **11.** *and that whoever does not fall down and worship will be thrown into a blazing furnace.* **12.** *But there are some Jews whom you have set over the affairs of the province of Babylon–Shadrach, Meshach and Abednego–who pay no attention to you, Your Majesty. They neither serve your gods nor worship the image of gold you have set up.'* **13.** *Furious with rage, Nebuchadnezzar summoned Shadrach, Meshach, and Abednego. So* *these men were brought before the king,* **14.** *and Nebuchadnezzar said to them, 'Is it true, Shadrach, Meshach, and Abednego, that you do not serve my gods or worship the image of gold I have set up?* **15.** *Now when you hear the sound of the horn, flute, zither, lyre, harp, pipe and all kinds of music, if you are ready to fall down and worship the image I made, very good. But if you do not worship it, you will be thrown immediately into a blazing furnace. Then what god will be able to rescue you from my hand?'* **16.** *Shadrach, Meshach, and Abednego replied to him, 'King Nebuchadnezzar, we do not need to defend ourselves before you in this matter.* **17.** *If we are thrown into the blazing furnace, the God we serve is able to deliver us from it, and he will deliver us from Your Majesty's hand.* **18.** *But even if he does not, we want you to know, Your Majesty, that we will not serve your gods or worship the image of gold you have set up."* (KJV).

The Bible explained the story of the three Hebrews who were living in a foreign land. And the king of the land had an idol that everyone must bow before the idol. These three young men have already built their trust and confidence in their own God. They believed, and they also established that God was greater than the idol that King Nebuchadnezzar had set before them.

Paul also admonished the church to pray for people in authority. Praying for people in power is vital in your day to day life. If you do not pray for them, they can bring up policies that will not favor you. They can bring up plans that will change the calendar of your life. That is why you need to pray for the men and women in the place of authority.

Prayer Points

- Father, I thank you for those in authority that they be saved.
- Father, in the name of Jesus, I pray for those in authority, that every decision they will make will favor the body of Christ.
- Father, in the name of Jesus, any man or woman in the place of authority will work together for the good of the gospel.
- Today as I appear before the authorities, they will grant me my heart desires.
- Those who are in charge to recommend me for promotion will not delay, they will act quickly.
- In the name of Jesus, the calendar of my testimony will not be tampered with by men in authority.
- In the name of Jesus, men in authority will not make me renounce my God.

1 Timothy 2:1, 2; "**1.** *I exhort therefore, that, first of all, supplications, prayers, intercessions,* *and giving of thanks, be made for all men;* **2.** *For kings, and for all that are in authority; that we may lead a quiet and peaceable life in all godliness and honesty"* (KJV). The word kings also imply Presidents and Governors. Whereas the phrase **'all that in authority'** means to those in a leadership position in your nation. In praying for your country, the scripture teaches you to pray for those in authority. You are to *pray that they lead a quiet and peaceable life in all godliness and honesty.* **1 Timothy 2:3, 4**; *"3. For this is good and acceptable in the sight of God our Saviour;* **4.** *Who will have all men to be saved, and to come unto the knowledge of the truth"* (KJV). *The reason for the prayer for those in authority is for their salvation because God's desire is for all men to be saved.* **2 Peter 3:9**; *"The Lord is not slack concerning his promise, as some men count slackness; but is long suffering to us-ward, not willing that any should perish, but that all should come to repentance"* (KJV).

Praying for those in authority is God's will for all men to be saved. These 'men' include all Presidents, State Governors, Local Government leaders, and all those in leadership positions. Men such as **Joseph of Arimathaea, Nicodemus, and Cornelius**, who received salvation, are good examples of men in authority or leadership positions. **John 19:38, 39**; *"38. And after this Joseph of Arimathaea, being a disciple of Jesus,* *but secretly for fear of the Jews, besought Pilate that he might take away the body of Jesus: and Pilate gave him leave. He came therefore, and took the body of Jesus.* **39.** *And there came also Nicodemus, which at the first came to Jesus by night, and brought a mixture of myrrh and aloes, about an hundred pound weight"* (KJV). Joseph of Arimathaea and Nicodemus were leaders in authority. Cornelius was also a military leader who received the gospel.

Act 10:1, 45; *"***1.** *There was a certain man in Caesarea called Cornelius, a centurion of the band called the Italian band...* **45.** *And they of the circumcision which believed were astonished, as many as came with Peter, because that on the Gentiles also was poured out the gift of the Holy Ghost"* (KJV). Other examples include **Act 13:7**; *"Which was with the* **deputy of the country, Sergius Paulus, a prudent man***; who called for Barnabas and Saul, and desired to hear the word of God".* **Acts 13:12;** *"Then the deputy, when he saw what was done, believed, being astonished at the doctrine of the Lord".* **Acts 18:8**; *"And* **Crispus, the chief ruler of the synagogue***, believed on the Lord with all his house; and many of the Corinthians hearing believed, and were baptized".* **Acts 28:7**; *"In the same quarters were possessions of the* **chief man of the island, whose name was Publius***; who received us, and lodged us three days courteously"* (KJV).

The apparent reasons scripture gave to pray for those in power is for the salvation of their soul so they can lead with godliness and honesty. Also, that they are not used as tools by the enemy against you, the believer.

Prayer to Obtain Favor from Authority

Esther 5:1–8; "**1.** *On the third day Esther put on her royal robes and stood in the inner court of the palace, in front of the king's hall. The king was sitting on his royal throne in the hall, facing the entrance.* **2.** *When he saw Queen Esther standing in the court, he was pleased with her and held out to her the gold scepter that was in his hand. So Esther approached and touched the tip of the scepter.* **3.** *Then the king asked, 'What is it, Queen Esther? What is your request? Even up to half the kingdom, it will be given you.'* **4.** *'If it pleases the king,' replied Esther, 'let the king, together with Haman, come today to a banquet I have prepared for him.'* **5.** *'Bring Haman at once,' the king said, 'so that we may do what Esther asks.' So the king and Haman went to the banquet Esther had prepared.* **6.** *As they were drinking wine, the king again asked Esther, 'Now what is your petition? It will be given you. And what is your request? Even up to half the kingdom, it will be granted.'* **7.** *Esther replied, 'My petition and my* *request is this:* **8.** *If the king regards me with favor and if it pleases the king to grant my petition and fulfill my request, let the king and Haman come tomorrow to the banquet I will prepare for them. Then I will answer the king's question'."* (KJV).

The Bible explained in detail the challenge the children of Israel found themselves. And God arranged a young woman called **Esther**, who will set them free from the challenge. There was a man who hated the children of Israel, and **Esther** came to their rescue. The Bible says she found favor in the eyes of the king.

Prayer Points

- Father, I receive favor wherever I go in the name of Jesus.
- As I stand before men in authority today, they will favor me in the name of Jesus.
- Men in authority will harken to my voice today in the name of Jesus.
- Every decision that is made in the place of authority will favor me in the name of Jesus.
- The favor of God will make me sit with those in authority in the name of Jesus.
- As Esther found favor in the eyes of the king, today, I will find favor in the eyes of those in authority.

Prayer brings holy boldness and favor. **Acts 4:29–33**; *"***29.** *And now, Lord, behold their threatenings: and grant unto thy servants, that with all boldness they may speak thy word,* **30.** *By stretching forth thine hand to heal; and that signs and wonders may be done by the name of thy holy child Jesus.* **31.** *And when they had prayed, the place was shaken where they were assembled together; and they were all filled with the Holy Ghost,* **and they spake the word of God with boldness***.* **32.** *And the multitude of them that believed were of one heart and of one soul: neither said any of them that ought of the things which he possessed was his own; but they had all things common.* **33.** *And with great power gave the apostles witness of the resurrection of the Lord Jesus: and great grace was upon them all"* (KJV).

That said, Christians often pray amiss. They pray to God to move in the nation by *pleading with an angry God to turn from His impending judgment and have mercy*. That is the wrong way to pray, which can open the door to incorrect results. There is the right way to pray for your nation. Firstly, you need to recognize that God is not **angry anymore**. The war between God and man is over as proclaimed by the angels at the birth of Jesus. **Luke 2:14**; says, *"Glory to God in the highest, and on earth peace, good will toward men."* (KJV).

The angels' proclamation does not mean from then on peace would reign on earth, and wars between men would cease. That certainly has not happened. They were proclaiming the end of the war between God and man. Jesus paid a price that is infinitely greater than the sins of the whole human race. God loves the world, not only the Church but the world. He's already paid for their sins as the Scriptures say in **1 John 2:2**; *"And he is the propitiation for our sins: and not for ours only, but also for the sins of the whole world."* (KJV).

Therefore, His mercy is now extended to all men, not the judgment you read about in the Old Testament. In the Old Testament, God's punishment was poured out on individuals and entire nations. In the New Testament, God's judgment was poured out on Jesus. Now, God's mercy and grace are yours. Through His mercy, you avoid getting the bad things you deserve, and through His grace, you receive the good things you do not deserve. The ***nearly-too-good-to-be-true*** news of the Gospel is that you do not get what you deserve; you get what you believe.

Jesus has made all that God is and has available to you, and it is through faith that you access that grace. **Romans 5:2**; *"By whom also we have access by faith into this grace wherein we stand and rejoice in hope of the glory of God"* (KJV). So, the typical Christian is making intercession to an angry God, asking Him to turn from His fierce wrath, but that is the wrong way to pray. I can hear you say, "But precisely that's what people did in the Old Testament!" That is true, but there is a significant difference between the Old and New Covenant, which is Jesus. Jesus has forever changed the way you approach God and how you appropriate His favor.

As New Testament believers, you should approach God differently. **Galatians 3:19**; refers to Moses as a mediator. *"Wherefore then serveth the law? It was added because of transgressions, till the seed should come to whom the promise was made; and it was ordained by angels in the hand of a mediator"* (KJV). The dictionary defines a mediator as 'someone who seeks to resolve differences between two or more conflicting parties.' It was appropriate for Moses to act as a mediator because Jesus had not yet come, and the atonement for man's sins had not been made. God and man were not yet reconciled. But now, because of Jesus, God has been reconciled to man.

All that is left is for man to be reconciled to God, which should be your message. **2 Corinthians 5:19, 20**; *"***19.** t*o wit, that God was in Christ, reconciling the world unto himself, not imputing their trespasses unto them; and hath committed unto us the word of reconciliation.* **20.** *Now then we are ambassadors for Christ, as though God did beseech you by us: we pray you in Christ's stead, be ye reconciled to God"* (KJV). To approach God as an adversary who is ready to destroy you is to approach God without Jesus. It does not honor the mediation that Jesus purchased. **1 Timothy 2:5** says, *"For there is one God, and one mediator between God and men, the man Christ Jesus."* (KJV).

When Jesus became your Mediator, He put all other mediators out of business. In the days of Moses, it was appropriate and necessary for him to act as a mediator and intercede for his nation, pleading with God to turn from his wrath. Why, because Jesus had not yet come and taken His place as the only Mediator. Now that Jesus has come and has paid for the sins of the whole world, it is wrong to continue to pray the way Moses did. It is against everything Christ accomplished. In other words, it is **anti-Christ**. I know those words are strong, but they are the truth.

How then should a New Testament Believer Intercede for their Nation?

Start by praising God for what He has already accomplished through Jesus. Then take your place in what Christ has already done. Use your authority as a believer to speak God's blessing over your nation instead of the curses that Christians so often pronounce. It is that simple. There is a tremendous authority given to you if you will use it, and there is incredible power in the blessings you received. God will not force Himself or His blessings on you.

You obtain His blessings through faith. Without a change in your heart and a change in the direction you are headed, you will forsake your mercies **(Jonah 2:8)** and reap death instead of life **(Romans. 6:16). Jonah 2:8**; *"They that observe lying vanities forsake their own mercy"* (KJV). **Romans 6:16**; *"Know ye not, that to whom ye yield yourselves servants to obey, his servants ye are to whom ye obey; whether of sin unto death, or of obedience unto righteousness?"* (KJV).

Men are in control of the earth (**psalm 115:16**; *"The heaven, even the heavens, are the LORD'S: but the earth hath he given to the children of men"*) (KJV). So for God to interfere in the affairs of the earth, he needs a man who will exercise his given authority by Christ (**Matthew 16:19**; *"And I will give unto thee the keys of the kingdom of heaven: and whatsoever thou shalt bind on earth shall be bound in heaven: and whatsoever thou shalt loose on earth shall be loosed in heaven"*) (KJV). Likewise, for Satan to operate, he needs you to use your authority negatively; **Proverbs 18:20**; *"***18.** A man's belly shall be satisfied with the fruit of his mouth; and with the increase of his lips shall he be filled.* **20.** *Death and life are in the power of the tongue: and they that love it shall eat the fruit thereof.* (KJV).

CHAPTER FIVE

PRAYING FOR INTERVENTION AND TO OVERCOME FEAR

DANIEL 6:1–16

In Daniel 6:1–16, "**1.** *It pleased Darius to set over the kingdom an hundred and twenty princes, which should be over the whole kingdom;* **2.** *And over these three presidents; of whom Daniel was first: that the princes might give accounts unto them, and the king should have no damage.* **3.** *Then this Daniel was preferred above the presidents and princes, because an excellent spirit was in him; and the king thought to set him over the whole realm.* **4.** *Then the presidents and princes sought to find* *occasion against Daniel concerning the kingdom; but they could find none occasion nor fault; forasmuch as he was faithful, neither was there any error or fault found in him.* **5.** *Then said these men, we shall not find any occasion against this Daniel, except we find it against him concerning the law of his God.* **6.** *Then these presidents and princes assembled together to the king, and said thus unto him, King Darius, live for ever.* **7.** *All the presidents of the kingdom, the governors, and the princes, the counsellors, and the captains, have consulted together to establish a royal statute, and to make a firm decree, that whosoever shall ask a petition of any God or man for thirty days, save of thee, O king, he shall be cast into the den of lions.* **8.** *Now, O king, establish the decree, and sign the writing, that it be not changed, according to the law of the Medes and Persians, which altereth not.* **9.** *Wherefore king Darius signed the writing and the decree.* **10.** *Now when Daniel knew that the writing was signed, he went into his house; and his windows being open in his chamber toward Jerusalem, he kneeled upon his knees three times a day, and prayed, and gave thanks before his God, as he did aforetime.* **11.** *Then these men assembled, and found Daniel praying and making supplication before his God.* **12.** *Then they came near, and spake before the king concerning the king's decree; Hast thou not signed a decree, that every man that shall* *ask a petition of any God or man within thirty days, save of thee, O king, shall be cast into the den of lions? The king answered and said, The thing is true, according to the law of the Medes and Persians, which altereth not.* **13.** *Then answered they and said before the king, That Daniel, which is of the children of the captivity of Judah, regardeth not thee, O king, nor the decree that thou hast signed, but maketh his petition three times a day.* **14.** *Then the king, when he heard these words, was sore displeased with himself, and set his heart on Daniel to deliver him: and he laboured till the going down of the sun to deliver him.* **15.** *Then these men assembled unto the king, and said unto the king, Know, O king, that the law of the Medes and Persians is, That no decree nor statute which the king establisheth may be changed.* **16.** *Then the king commanded, and they brought Daniel, and cast him into the den of lions. Now the king spake and said unto Daniel, Thy God whom thou servest continually, he will deliver thee"* (KJV).

Daniel was a man who believed in the God of Israel. He was a man from the tribe of Judah. Daniel believed that the only way to communicate with God Almighty is through prayers. Daniel still prayed in season and out of season despite the King's decree that prayers be offered to only the gods of that particular kingdom. Men rose against him to see that he was destroyed. But God intervened on his behalf. Prayer is not just telling God your needs because He already knows them; **Matthew 6:32**; *"(For after all these things do the Gentiles seek:) for your heavenly Father knoweth that ye have need of all these things"* (KJV).

Instead, prayer is getting God to intervene in your situations based on His Word, through the exercise of the exceeding power he has made available in the believer **Ephesians 3:20**; *"Now unto him that is able to do exceeding abundantly above all that we ask or think, according to the power that worketh in us"*. **Ephesians 1:9**; *"Having made known unto us the mystery of his will, according to his good pleasure which he hath purposed in himself"* (KJV).

For instance, when brother Peter was held up in prison, the church never ceased praying for him; **Acts 12: 5–11**; *"***5.** *Peter therefore was kept in prison: but prayer was made without ceasing of the church unto God for him.* **6.** *And when Herod would have brought him forth, the same night Peter was sleeping between two soldiers, bound with two chains: and the keepers before the door kept the prison.* **7.** *And, behold, the angel of the Lord came upon him, and a light shined in the prison: and he smote Peter on the side, and raised him up, saying, Arise up quickly. And his chains fell off from his hands.* **8.** *And the angel said unto him, Gird thyself, and bind on thy sandals. And so he did. And he saith* *unto him, Cast thy garment about thee, and follow me. 9. And he went out, and followed him; and wist not that it was true which was done by the angel; but thought he saw a vision. 10. When they were past the first and the second ward, they came unto the iron gate that leadeth unto the city; which opened to them of his own accord: and they went out, and passed on through one street; and forthwith the angel departed from him. 11. And when Peter was come to himself, he said, Now I know of a surety, that the Lord hath sent his angel, and hath delivered me out of the hand of Herod, and from all the expectation of the people of the Jews"* (KJV).

It is not true that everything will be delivered to you on a platter of gold as a believer. Things do not just happen; they are made to happen. Being a believer gives you an edge over the opposition and does not automatically exempt you from life issues or warfare. In your Christian walk with God, warfare is inevitable, but victory is guaranteed. **1 John 5:4**; *"For whatsoever is born of God overcometh the world: and this is the victory that overcometh the world, even our faith"* (KJV). **John 16:33**; *"These things I have spoken unto you, that in me ye might have peace. In the world ye shall have tribulation: but be of good cheer; I have overcome the world"* (KJV).

So, victory is your heritage. As long as you are still breathing, the battles of life are not over.

So, you cannot wish problems away nor accept the status quo, but you must rise to the challenge and stop tolerating failure and mishaps. Stop putting up with pains, lack, and want. It is a strategy of the enemy to make you feel you cannot handle the issue. It is time to rise again. Champions are not those who never fail, but those who fail and refuse to remain a failure. So, get up on your feet and stand your ground against the devil in prayers to secure your glorious destiny in God.

Prayer Points

- Every plot of men to silence me from service to my God will not come to pass in the name of Jesus.
- Father intervene over my situation as you intervened over Daniels case in Jesus name.
- I command every angel assigned to work with me to silence those who want to harm me in the name of Jesus.
- Every voice that is rising to destroy me hear the word of the Lord; my God will deliver me from you in Jesus name.
- As Daniel overcame the plot to destroy him, I will overcome every plot of destruction in Jesus name.

- Every strange voice that is spoken for my downfall, hear the voice of the Lord, it will not come to pass in Jesus name.

Prayer to Overcome Fear

2 Timothy 1:7; *"For God hath not given us the spirit of fear; but of power, and of love, and of a sound mind"* (KJV). In his letter to Timothy, Paul reminds him that God did not give believers the spirit of fear, but the spirit of sound mind and boldness. As a believer, you must not condone fear in your life because fear is the opposite of unbelief. The devil loves it when you tremble and quake with fear (anxiety, apprehension, and worry) over something that does not exist – just 'a shadow' of giant/challenges itself.

Shadows have a way of twisting things out of perspective. Shadows can make 'mountains out of molehills.' But the reactions they often cause can be potentially devastating. Thus, a believer should read, study, and meditate on God's word and pray as a key to living a victorious Christian life. If you fail to discipline yourself in this way, you will find yourself at a loss when confronted with life's challenges. When you are confronted with 'giants' in trials and tests, the enemy is taunting you to intimidate you. Satan exaggerates his powers and abilities and raises doubts in your mind concerning God's character (willingness or ability) to help you.

Satan's goal is to cause you to be *"dismayed and much afraid"* **1 Samuel 17:2–11.** You are often overcome by the enemy's lies and taunts that you are defeated even before you try to fight (pray). The devil knows that if he can get you to yield to fear and remain in fear, he will win the battle because fear confuses your thinking and causes you to act contrary to God's word. The devil will gain the advantage over you if you are ignorant of his schemes (modus operandi or mode of operation). The only way to recognize Satan's plans and successfully stand against the devil is through your knowledge of God's word (your identity with Christ Jesus) and prayer.

Where Does God's Word Come in Receiving/ Harvesting?

The enemy's primary strength lies in his ability to deceive and distract and lure a believer away from God's word and faith. Once he can sow the seed of doubt concerning God's word, he will defeat you. But when you hold the enemy in the realm of faith and believing by declaring God's word without wavering, the enemy will be of no match for the power of God's word made available through you. When God's word is planted deep in your heart, it becomes your weapon and then spoken from your mouth in faith, it becomes a powerful force.

It is not quoting just any scripture that will produce the power to overcome your life challenges, but in speaking the right scripture to get the job done. **Ephesians 6:17, 18**; *"17. And take the helmet of salvation, and the sword of the Spirit, which is **the word of God**: 18. Praying always with all prayer and supplication in the Spirit, and watching thereunto with all perseverance and supplication for all saints"* (KJV). In his letter to the Corinthian church, Paul reminded them about the importance of believing and then speaking what you believe. **2 Corinthian 4:13**; *"We having the same spirit of faith, according as **it is written**, I **believed**, and therefore have I spoken; we also believe, and therefore **speak**"* (KJV).

Jesus also said in **Mark 11:23**; *"For verily I say unto you, That whosoever shall say unto this mountain, Be thou removed, and be thou cast into the sea; and shall not doubt in his heart, but shall believe that those things which he saith shall come to pass; he shall have whatsoever he saith"* (KJV). Now that you know the principle of 'believing and speaking' is essential, use the right ammunition and scriptures with your weapon of believing and speaking God's word to reap bountifully in prayer, discarding fear. God's word and prayer go hand in hand in achieving answers to your requests. Sometimes believers want to have a long prayer session about something they are going through – which is very good.

Still, it should not take the time of exercising their God-given authority in the situation. **Philippians 4:19**; *"But my God shall supply all your need according to his riches in glory by Christ Jesus"* (KJV). For instance, by faith, you may declare this scripture or similar scripture continuously in line with your condition instead of praying for hours. Prayer is powerful, and believers should be doing more of it. But sometimes you do not need long hours of prayer but step out in faith and do what you know how to do. Prayer plays a vital role in the life of a Christian. A believer needs a strong prayer life to maintain a spiritual walk with God and stay attuned to His spirit.

However, praying cannot take the place of obedience to step out in faith and act on God's spoken word. God's word must be spoken for it to be effective. It is good to read, study, and meditate on God's word, but the word that remains unspoken will be ineffective against life challenges. Therefore, a believer should activate the weapons of warfare in the face of trials and temptations, saying *"it is written..."* to overcome circumstances in boldness and continual confession of God's word.

God is God – He was, is, and always will be Almighty God. As a believer today, you should be quick to stand against the world's oppression that tries to creep into the church and your personal life. Be it sin, sickness, disease, or poverty, you should resist it with God's word on your lips, refusing to be defeated or give up and quit in prayer. Jesus demonstrated it while he was in the boat with his disciples. He was at peace with himself. You may indeed encounter a lot of challenges and troubles in life. Still, God's word is more significant than any problem you may be going through right now.

My prayer for someone reading this book right now is that the word of God will swallow every challenge you are going through in Jesus name.

Prayer Points

- Father, in the name of Jesus, I receive boldness to fight against the spirit of fear in the name of Jesus.
- Whatsoever, that is threatening my peace hear the word of the Lord, I will overcome you in the name of Jesus.
- Every storm of fear blowing towards me be still in the name of Jesus.
- Father, in the name of Jesus, chase away those who create fear around me in Jesus name.
- Friends or family members whose intention is to clothe me with the spirit of fear, father keep them far from me in Jesus name.

- Unpalatable situations around me hear the word of the Lord; you will bow to my command in the name of Jesus.
- My ears from today will no longer listen to the voice of fear again in the name of Jesus.
- I refuse to be under the preachers of fear of this age in the name of Jesus.

CHAPTER SIX

PRAYER FOR WISDOM AND KNOWLEDGE

JAMES 1:5

"If any of you lack wisdom, let him ask of God, that giveth to all men liberally, and upbraideth not; and it shall be given him" (KJV).

Proverbs **22:3**; *"A prudent man foreseeth the evil, and hideth himself: but the simple pass on, and are punished"* (KJV). Wisdom is far better than anointing. With wisdom, you will know when to leave the stage. You will know by revelation to quit anything you are doing. Wisdom makes you see ahead and gives you a solution to problems. It also makes you know that not all doors are your doors, no matter how beautiful they are. A man of wisdom is never caught up with surprises. In **John 7:1**; *"After these things Jesus walked in Galilee: for he would not walk in Jewry, because the Jews sought to kill him"* (KJV). They sought to kill Jesus, but wisdom made him withdraw from that environment immediately. If you must be ahead in this present age, then you need to ask God for wisdom.

Prayer Points

- Father, in the name of Jesus Christ, clothe my heart with your wisdom.
- Father, in the name of Jesus, I receive wisdom to be ahead in my place of work.
- Father, in the name of Jesus, I receive wisdom to see ahead of every situation.
- Father, in the name of Jesus, I receive wisdom to solve every crisis ahead of me.
- I receive wisdom to be ahead of my peers.
- By wisdom, I stand against all challenges ahead of me in the name of Jesus.
- By wisdom, I will not fall into the trap of adversaries, in the name of Jesus.
- By wisdom, my mouth will speak solutions into the lives of men in the name of Jesus.

Prayer for Knowledge

Ephesians 1:7; *"That the God of our Lord Jesus Christ, the Father of glory, may give unto you the spirit of wisdom and revelation in the knowledge of him:"* (KJV). **Knowledge IS HEALING**. The day a scripture is unfolded to you, you are no longer ignorant of that scripture. Nobody can interpret that scripture to manipulate you any longer. Meaning you are healed from ignorance. For instance the theme of **Isaiah 53** was transgressions, sins and iniquity. A major problem is the language issue. Let's do a little exegesis;

Isaiah 53: 4. *"Surely he hath borne our griefs, and carried our sorrows: yet we did esteem him stricken, smitten of God, and afflicted. **5.** But he was wounded for our transgressions; he was bruised for our iniquities: the chastisement of our peace was upon him; and with his stripes we are healed. **6.** All we like sheep have gone astray; we have turned everyone to his own way; and the LORD hath laid on him the iniquity of us all".* (KJV)

Note:

- Grief's
- Sorrows
- 'By his stripes, we are healed…'

The Bible translators were implying that Jesus bore the sicknesses. The reason is that they could not translate it well. The word sorrow is how the Greek translated it and where we have the word leper.

In **Matthew 8:17** *That it might be fulfilled which was spoken by Esaias the prophet, saying, Himself took our infirmities, and bare our sicknesses.* Matthew wrote this account after Jesus had risen from the dead. In Jesus' healing ministry, He was not bearing people's sickness on his body. This prophecy in Isaiah 53 was about Jesus **sufferings**. It could not have been referring to His healing ministry. So, Jesus' healing ministry was to single Him out that He will bear the **sorrow** and **grief** of man, and a sign that He is Christ, the messiah - that is what Matthew meant.

Peter in **Acts 2:22** wrote "*Ye men of Israel, hear these words; Jesus of Nazareth, a man approved of God among you by miracles and wonders and signs, which God did by him in the midst of you, as ye yourselves also know*": He says God approved him. Jesus was singled out by God anointing Him in **Luke 4:18, 19.**

Peter explains Isaiah 53 better; he said **Jesus bore our sins**. No apostle ever said Jesus died for physical sickness. However, based on the redemptive work, healing is available to you. The work of redemption has brought healing to your bodies.

Isaiah 53:10. *Yet it pleased the LORD to bruise him; he hath put him to grief: when thou shalt make his soul an offering for sin, he shall see his seed, he shall prolong his days, and the pleasure of the LORD shall prosper in his hand.* **11.** *He shall see of the travail of his soul, and shall be satisfied: by his knowledge shall my righteous servant justify many; for he shall bear their iniquities.* **12.** *Therefore will I divide him a portion with the great, and he shall divide the spoil with the strong; because he hath poured out his soul unto death: and he was numbered with the transgressors; and he bare the sin of many, and made intercession for the transgressors.*

God put Him to grief. Grief is where we have the word sickness. The phrase 'His soul' means it is beyond the physical body. The essence there was an offering for sin (see **Romans 5:16-19).** His soul was poured to death. So, the scriptures are written in the light of the sufferings of Christ and the glory that should follow. Another key thing in **Isaiah 53:12** is 'identification'. The sinner is justified, and the transgressor is made righteous by the offering of Jesus Christ. This is where Paul's theology is expanded from. When Jesus was talking about sinners, He said that **'he that is whole does not need a physician'** - He was not talking about sickness but sin.

In Isaiah 53, the words used refer to physical sickness or disease. However, the interpretation of these words does not mean physical sickness but sin. Hence the statement 'knowledge is healing'. The sufferings of Christ and glory that should follow will be sufferings from sin. We have not substantiated that Jesus bore and suffered for sickness. We had evidence He became sin, but none that He became sick. Jesus' suffering for sin makes divine healing available, but Jesus' suffering for sin is not Jesus' suffering for sickness. **Psalm 110:1** and **Isaiah 53** carry the weight of redemption. Your understanding of them will help your Christian walk.

The body has changed its identity; it has been paid for - **1 Corinthians 6:19, 20; Romans 12:1** - Holy and acceptable to God. The nature of the body did not change because of redemption but will only at the resurrection. You can be healed - **Philippians 2:25-26**. The word 'healed' means to cure. It was used well in Matthew, Book of Acts and once in **John 5:10.** Divine healing is a combination of Faith, Food and Common sense. Jesus' suffering for your sin makes divine healing available to you. Thus you know how to receive and therefore walk in divine healing. As your body can be healed anytime it has pain and sickness.

Also, according to **Matthew, Mark, Luke 16:16-17,** and **John 8:29**, by knowledge, Peter called Jesus thou art Christ, the Son of the living God in the gospels. No other apostle among the twelve apostles of the lamb called Him the Son of the living God, not until Peter opened his mouth by knowledge. When Paul said, let God's word dwell in you richly; it merely means having the sacred knowledge of God inside you. Prayer becomes a worthless religious exercise without the 'Word'. **1 John 5:14**; *"And this is the confidence that we have in him, that, if we ask any thing according to his will, he heareth us:* (KJV).

Lack of Word preparation is the reason for your frustrations in prayer. Your training in the Word can secure your approval for your request even before you speak. When your heart is filled with the relevant scriptures that help you communicate your desires effectively, your prayers become effectual and makes tremendous power available. Before you engage in any prayer session as an individual and as a church, you need to sit down and prepare, like you are going to court. Be organized and write down your prayer points and scriptures that commit God to grant your desires and stop playing religion. There may be no one near you when you are confronted with the hottest battles in life, and if you do not know how to connect to God, what becomes of you as a believer? So, brace up and have a Word-stuffed heart to maintain a hotline communication with God.

Colossians 3:16; *"Let the word of Christ dwell in you richly in all wisdom; teaching and admonishing one another in psalms and hymns and spiritual songs, singing with grace in your hearts to the Lord"* (KJV). Prayer is communication, not emotional displays. Your tear does not move God; He is only moved when you ask according to His will. So, all you need is the right words, and your communication with Him will be through. The Word is the only language He understands and permits Him to intervene in your case. **Psalm 138:2**; *"I will worship toward thy holy temple, and praise thy name for thy loving kindness and for thy truth: for thou hast magnified thy word above all thy name"* (KJV).

It is God's Word that makes one outstanding in Christianity, not religious exercises. Many prayer warriors are weary, but a Word Warrior is a conqueror. When you are Wordless, your prayers cannot be genuine. You will be under pressure. That is why you get tired quickly when you engage in prayer sessions. Have you ever asked yourself why you have been praying on the same issue for over six months or a year and more without getting an answer? And you never bothered to sit down and ask yourself, what am I doing wrong? It is God's word that connects you. God's word is the power that flows through the cable line of the prayer, which brings about resounding results.

Isaiah 43:26; *"Put me in remembrance: let us plead together: declare thou, that thou mayest be justified"* (KJV). So, until you remind Him of His Word that commits Him to your breakthrough, your prayers will continue to remain unanswered. Effectual prayer begins with Word preparation, but it delivers through a sound-connection with the Father. After locating God's will concerning your situation, the next thing to do is apply the Word for an efficient result. Prayer will be unproductive without faith. Faith is the ticket to take delivery of anything. You do not pray for faith; you cultivate faith by staying in the Word through meditation until the assurance of its reality is established in your heart, before presenting your request.

Faith is the switch button that turns on the Word, which is the power that flows through the cable of prayer to give you an expected result. Hence the Word can only produce a result when faith is present. **Romans 10:17**; *"So then faith cometh by hearing, and hearing by the word of God"* (KJV). Once faith is established, you can be sure of results when you pray; **James 1:6, 7**; *"6. But let him ask in faith, nothing wavering. For he that wavereth is like a wave of the sea driven with the wind and tossed. 7. For let not that man think that he shall receive any thing of the Lord"* (KJV).

God's Word grants you the audience before Him, while your FAITH motivates Him to act on your behalf. So, it is you who determines whether your prayer gets answered or not and not God because He is constant in all His ways. **Matthew 6:7**; *"But when ye pray, use not vain repetitions, as the heathen do: for they think that they shall be heard for their much speaking. **8.** Be not ye therefore like unto them: for your Father knoweth what things ye have need of, before ye ask him"*. (KJV). So, effectual prayer is not in many words. Only meaningful words give you the audience before God. You are heard by target words that are shot as arrows that cannot miss its target. Prayer is saying the right thing. Vain repetitions and idle expressions (words) are why many remain in prayers for days and still come out without results.

That said, Philip asked the centurion man do you understand what you are reading? And the man said not until someone who knows explains. Friends, you may read the Bible and not understand what is written therein. You need the knowledge to explain it. knowledge comes from above and is different from academic knowledge. When Jesus took the scroll in Luke's gospel and explained it in a simple term, the Pharisees were amazed and astonished. It is the knowledge that gives birth to revelation. Without knowledge, there cannot be a revelation. In his letters, Brother Paul kept emphasizing *'that you may know'*, the exceeding power, and might of God's greatness. When you know, things will unlock and open itself to you, and situations will bow.

Prayer Points

- I receive knowledge to handle my day to day affairs of life.
- I receive the ability to know; to unlock the unknown.
- I receive knowledge of God to quench the battles of my life in the name of Jesus.
- From today, through the knowledge of God, nothing will ever hurt me again.
- In the name of Jesus, by knowledge of God, my body is no longer a dwelling place for sickness.
- By knowledge of God, I will excel in everything I lay my hands to do.

CHAPTER SEVEN

THE PLACE OF THANKSGIVING AND PRAISE IN PRAYER

Based on your knowledge of reading this book, prayer will no longer be a fruitless religious activity but an active, productive, heart-to-heart communication with God. This chapter will show you how to take delivery of your answered prayers after engaging your communication links with the Father.

1 Timothy 2:1; *"I exhort therefore, that, first of all, supplications, prayers, intercessions, and giving of thanks, be made for all men"* (KJV). **1 Corinthians 14:14–17**; *"14. For if I pray in an* *unknown tongue, my spirit prayeth, but my understanding is unfruitful.* **15.** *What is it then?* ***I will pray with the spirit****, and I will pray with the understanding also: I will sing with the spirit, and I will sing with the understanding also.* **16.** *Else when thou shalt bless with the spirit, how shall he that occupieth the room of the unlearned say Amen at thy giving of thanks, seeing he understandeth not what thou sayest* **17.** *For thou verily givest thanks well, but the other is not edified"* (KJV).

Philippians 4:6; *"Be careful for nothing; but in everything by prayer and supplication with **thanksgiving** let your requests be made known unto God"* (KJV). **Colossians 4:2**; *"Continue in prayer, and watch in the same with **thanksgiving"***. **1 Thessalonians 5:17, 18**, *"***17.** *Pray without ceasing.* **18.** *In everything **give thanks**: for this is the will of God in Christ Jesus concerning you"* (KJV). Giving of thanks is a sign of gratitude and means thankfulness. Thanksgiving is the last discussion after your supplication and prayer with the Father.

How do we give thanks as believers?

Ephesians 6:18; *"Praying always with **all prayer** and supplication **in the Spirit**, and watching thereunto with all perseverance and supplication for all saints;* (KJV). From the Bible references, **1 Corinthians 14:16, 17**, **Colossians 3:16**; brother Paul says *"...I will pray with the spirit..."* Thus, *how to give thanks* is also done IN THE SPIRIT according to **Ephesians** 6:18 *"...**all prayer and supplication in the Spirit**..."* – All prayers also include thanksgiving. Most people do not know that a grateful heart is not just a nice experience to have or a desirable attitude–there is spiritual power in praise and thanksgiving.

As Christians, you are called to unleash the power of praise and thanksgiving every day. You are to unleash the power to defeat the devil and unlock victory. It is wrong to think and treat praise as what you do after getting what you are believing or praying God to receive. Andrew Wommack says, *"Praise isn't like the caboose that just follows what happens, but it's more like the engine of a train that makes things happen."* Kenneth Copeland says, *"Praise is the big gun of faith."*

The devil wants to keep you from thinking about praise and thanksgiving while you are in the process of believing because he knows it's an important key to breakthrough. Where there are thanksgiving and praise, doubt, grumbling or murmuring will have no room in you. Remember when Paul and Silas were locked up in the bowels of a prison? Things looked grim. Most people would be begging and pleading with God to get them out or considering all the ways they served Him and wondering how they could deserve what was happening.

Instead, Paul and Silas "were praying and singing to God." **Acts 16:25 (NIV).** The result? *"All the prison doors flew open, and everyone's chains came loose"* **verse 26.** All because of praise and thanksgiving to God. Dr. Abel Damina said, *"Thanksgiving is not a precondition for God's blessing rather it is our ceaseless attitude to our Father's unconditional blessings. It is not a gift to God for blessings but a response to his blessings".* If you need to breakthrough, open the prison doors, and break chains, you will need to activate the power of praise and thanksgiving every day. Unleash the power of praise and thanksgiving with these truths, and you shall breakthrough, open prison doors, and loose chains.

Praise and Thanksgiving Balance the Scale

"Do not be anxious about anything, but in every situation, by prayer and petition, with thanksgiving, present your requests to God." **Philippians 4:6 (NIV).** Notice that **Philippians 4:6**; says you are to present your requests to God *"by prayer and petition, with thanksgiving."* You can often get so wrapped up in your needs and desires that your prayers can end up sounding like a long list of what you don't have, what you want and what you need without much time spent praising God whom you are petitioning. There is nothing wrong with asking for God's help, but you should

also be taking the time to thank God for everything He has done and is doing for you.

Praise and thanksgiving balance your prayer life scale and mean the difference between receiving and going without receiving. Do your praises equal your prayers? Is your scale balanced? Do not wait to offer praise and thanksgiving to God until things are just as you like them to be–praise Him in every situation. Praise Him for who He is and what He's done in your life. Praise Him that you are saved, delivered, and healed. Praise Him as your Creator, Restorer, Friend, Counsellor, and Comforter. Thank him for Christ's finished work (righteousness, justification, and sanctification), the unfinished work, and the ongoing work. There are so many reasons to be thankful to God every day. So, take the time to thank Him daily.

Praise and Thanksgiving Neutralize the Devil

"In everything give thanks: for this is the will of God in Christ Jesus concerning you." **1 Thessalonians 5:18 (KJV).** Have you ever wondered why the devil tries to get you to complain and grumble? He knows it is a strength sapper, a faith drainer, and a dream killer. More importantly, he does not want you to know that praise and thanksgiving neutralize him (the devil). Praise and thanksgiving are powerful spiritual weapons that come from a highly developed faith, and they are

often the final step before receiving from God. They are sure signs that you have faith in His Word, and have eradicated all unbelief, and have fixed your mind solely on His Word. That is a great place to be!

How does praise and thanksgiving give you strength?

They build your faith and keep you thinking right. When you slip into wrong thinking, Satan can gain access to your life. Praise and thanksgiving are vital weapons in your warfare against Satan and his forces. Exercise faith by keeping your lips oiled with thanksgiving and praise to God when things seem oblique and look contrary to what you believe. Refuse to be moved by the circumstances (mountain/ challenge) in front of you and continuously praise Him with your eyes fixated on His word to answer your prayers.

Praise and thanksgiving will always send the devil packing! The next time the devil tries to stifle your effectiveness, to drain you of the strength, wealth, and victory that are yours in Jesus, turn him back with those powerful weapons. Lift your hands, your voice, and your whole heart to God. Give Him praise and thanksgiving! When Satan starts shaking your mountain, do not retreat and run for cover. Speak to the mountain with the authority you have in the name of Jesus.

Then, when you are done with that, start to praise and shout the victory! **Psalm 22:3**; *"But You are holy, O You Who dwell in [the holy place where] the praises of Israel [are offered].* – **(AMPC).** Praise is not something you do when things are rosy. God is always worthy of your praise. The Bible says to offer the sacrifice of praise–that means when it feels like a tough thing to give. So, when you pray, *"enter into his gates WITH THANKSGIVING, and into his courts WITH PRAISE: be thankful unto him, and bless his name".* **Psalm 100:4** (KJV).

Praise and thanksgiving are integral parts of prayer. It involves you fellowshipping with God through your thanksgiving and praise. **Philippians 4:6** explains why you should mix thanksgiving with your prayers. Now that you know how to unleash the power of praise and thanksgiving, you can take these truths and put them in remembrance as you pray and engage in spiritual warfare. **Never underestimate the importance of praise and thanksgiving.** It is one of the most powerful spiritual weapons the believer has!

When you thank God for all His blessings, it refocuses your attention from the negative to positive things. Sure, you have problems as you live in a fallen world, but God is good, and God's goodness to you is greater than all the enemy's attacks. Brother Paul praised God after being beaten, stoned, whipped, and thrown in jail. Then he said these were but light afflictions that last for a moment, nothing to be compared to eternal gains. **2 Corinthians. 4:17, 18.** Paul understood that praise from a grateful heart has great power and builds you up spiritually; it serves as a source of strength and a powerful weapon against the devil, and it ministers to the Lord.

CONCLUSION

Prayer is a powerful weapon. But there is a right and a wrong way to pray. Like any powerful weapon, it may be useless without the proper instruction, or someone could get hurt. *The wrong prayer is not only ineffective; it can also release the power of the devil.*

I read in Andrew W. article about a teenager who felt ineffective in witnessing for the Lord and prayed and asked for the Lord to do whatever it takes to use him as an effective witness in his high school. He asked God to give him cancer and take his life if that was the only way he could show others God's power in his life. The next day the boy came down with leukemia. At his funeral, four of his classmates accepted Christ because of how he had dealt with the terminal illness.

At that time, the writer said he never knew that God had redeemed the believer from sickness because he had been taught that God controlled everything that happened to us in God's sovereignty. He fell hook, line, and sinker for this teaching and gave the tape to a close friend who accepted it as the truth to the point that she prayed the same prayer as the teenager. The next morning, she was rushed to the hospital and diagnosed with leukemia. At her funeral, four people accepted the Lord also.

Later, the writer understood that God did not answer those prayers by giving two teenagers leukemia. Certainly, God received a measure of glory when those eight people accepted the Lord, but God does not kill one of His children so that others can be saved. Satan is the killer who took advantage of the open doors these wrong prayers created. That is why it is important to know how to pray. About prayer, you must be guided through God's word.

You are taught how to pray consistently in the following scriptures: **1 Thessalonians 5:17**; *"Pray without ceasing"*. **Ephesians 6:12**; *"For we wrestle not against flesh and blood, but against principalities, against powers, against the rulers of the darkness of this world, against spiritual* *wickedness in high places"* **(KJV). Colossians 4:12**; *"Epaphras, who is one of you, a servant of Christ, saluteth you, always labouring fervently for you in prayers, that ye may stand perfect and complete in all the will of God"* (KJV).

Romans 12:12; *"Rejoicing in hope; patient in tribulation; continuing instant in prayer"* (KJV). Hence it is important to note that the epistles emphasize praying for the saints when praying for people. You admonished to pray for both the saints and those yet to hear the gospel (the non-believing people). **2 Corinthians 4:3, 4, Romans 10:14–17)** No one gets saved by prayer. Those yet to hear the gospel needs to hear and believe the gospel before they can be saved. Hence the need for the preacher to reach and be sent to them. It has been established that prayer is fellowship.

Jesus demonstrated this attitude in his ministry. You also have fellowship with your Father when you pray **(1 Corinthians 14:2)**. As seen in **1 Corinthians 14:18**, brother Paul prayed regularly in tongues. So, praying in the spirit goes beyond making requests. It is how you fellowship with your Father. Praying in the spirit helps you stand against the enemy as much as you build up yourself, and you are strengthened by prayer. Do not forget that supplication is done in the spirit. In the letters written to the churches in the epistles, prayer focuses on people and circumstances surrounding the gospel.

When you pray in the spirit, you pray more effectively and get results.

Thus, you are instructed to pray much in the spirit, and cultivating this act is very important as a believer. More so, most Christians long for peace and desire to live in perfect peace. However, **Isaiah 26:3** says, *"Thou wilt keep him in perfect peace, whose mind is stayed on thee: because he trusteth in thee."* (KJV). Hence, perfect peace comes from God, and from keeping your whole being fixated on God and trusting in Him. You have also learned that one of the greatest antidotes to fear and worry is thanksgiving and praise. Moreover, the name of Jesus is your heritage in God. In **John 16:24**; *"Hitherto have ye asked nothing IN MY NAME: ask, and ye shall receive, that your joy may be full"* (KJV).

So, the name is the authority seal that validates your request. The authority and power in the name of Jesus are what you release when you pray in His name. Brother Peter prayed for the lame man at the gate. *"Beautiful"*, he said in **Acts 3:6, 7;** *"**6.**... Silver and gold have I none; but such as I have give I thee: **In the name of Jesus Christ** of Nazareth rise up and walk. **7.** And he took him by the right hand and lifted him up: and immediately his feet and ankle bones received strength"* (KJV). So, whenever you pray to your father, you must expect to receive it.

REFERENCES FOR PRAYE

Prayers for Outreach

- 1 Thessalonians 1:5
- 1 Timothy 2:3–4
- Acts 26:18
- 1 Corinthians 13:10
- 1 Corinthians 13:12
- 2 Corinthians 10:5
- 1 Corinthians 15:2
- 2 Corinthians 11:3
- Ephesian 1:17
- Ephesian 1:18-19
- Ephesians 4:12
- Ephesian 4:13–14

- Philippians 1:11
- Colossians 1:9
- 1 Thessalonians 1:13
- 1 Thessalonians 3:10
- 2 Thessalonians 3:1
- 2 Thessalonians 3:3

Prayers for the Church

- 2 Corinthians 3:5, 6
- Romans 1:8
- 1 Corinthians 1:5
- Romans 5:1
- 1 Peter 1:3, 4
- 2 Peter 1:3
- Philippians 1:9, 10
- Philippians 1:11
- 1 Corinthians 2:5
- 1 Corinthians 2:12
- Ephesians 1:3
- Hebrews 10:14
- 2 Corinthians 10:8
- Ephesians 2:4–6
- Ephesians 2:18, 19
- Ephesians 3:16–19
- Philippians 2:13

- Philippians 4:19
- Colossians 1:12
- Hebrews 1:3
- Colossians. 1:13-14
- 1 Thessalonians 5:1–5
- 2 Thessalonians 1:11
- 2 Thessalonians 2:13, 14
- 2 Timothy 1:7
- Jude 24
- 2 Thessalonians 2:15
- Ephesians 4:1
- 2 Thessalonians 1:12
- 2 Peter 1:10
- 2 Peter 2:28
- 1 Corinthians 12:1
- 1 Corinthians 12:8
- 1 Thessalonians 5:19-20
- 1 Corinthians 12:25
- Ephesians 4:12
- Philemon 6
- 1 Corinthians 15:58
- Galatians 5:1
- 2 Timothy 1:13
- 2 Timothy 2:2
- 2 Timothy 2:15
- Philippians 1:9-10

- Philippians 1:27
- Philippians 1:28, 29
- 1 Thessalonians 5:23
- Philippians 2:2
- Philippians 2:16
- Colossians 1:10
- Colossians 1:11
- Colossians 2:7, 8
- Colossians 3:1, 2
- Colossians 4:12
- 1 Thessalonians 3:12, 13
- 1 Thessalonians 4:13–18
- 2 Thessalonians 3:5
- Jude 3

ABOUT THE AUTHOR

Abimbola O. Olagunju is a believer in the finished work of Christ and desires to see the truth lived out in believers. He is the founder of Hope for Missionaries, an NGO through which God brings smiles to the forgotten missionaries scattered around several villages in Nigeria and beyond through which God has loosened tightly knotted life challenges.

Prayer Harvest as a book is designed to create an awareness of the responsibility to all believers. It will bless you beyond your widest imaginations and seek to correct any misinformation by which your life might have been patterned. Just like any powerful weapon, without the proper instruction, it may be useless, or someone could get hurt. Wrong prayer is not only ineffective; it can also release the power of the devil. Just read with an open heart to Jesus.